The Way of Magic

Gordon Strong

SKYLIGHT
PRESS

First published in Great Britain in 2012 by Skylight Press,
210 Brooklyn Road, Cheltenham, Glos GL51 8EA

Cover photography by Matt Baldwin-Ives
Designed and typeset by Rebsie Fairholm
Publisher: Daniel Staniforth

www.skylightpress.co.uk

Printed and bound in Great Britain by Lightning Source, Milton Keynes. Typeset in Adobe Caslon Pro. Titles set in Ultimos Ritos, a font by Fernando Forero.

British Library Cataloguing in Publication Data.
A catalogue record for this book is available from the British Library.

ISBN 978-1-908011-53-4

Contents

Acknowledgements

As always I am indebted to Alan Richardson for continuing to encourage all my literary and magical endeavours – not only in correspondence but in other, invisible ways. He has always been an inspiration to me, as were the first magicians I met in those strange but eventful times over forty years ago.

In my own practice of magic I could not have attained the heights that I have without a High Priestess. I am eternally grateful to those who fulfilled this role and I respect their desire to remain anonymous. Through their vision the face of the Goddess shined upon me.

Finally, I would like to thank Rebsie and Daniel for their hard work, dedication and encouragement.

Foreword

To produce a work which is anything like a definitive account of magic would be not only presumptuous but impossible. All things change, and magic is no exception. All the writer upon the metaphysical arts can hope to do is illustrate and explain the principles he believes are essential to that discipline, and to share certain insights from his own experience. He will also be acutely aware that he follows a well-worn but sacred path. Agree he must with the words of Isaac Newton, 'If I have seen farther it is by standing on the shoulders of giants.'

Those who wish to study and take up the practice of magic (and there is little point in doing the one without the other) should be aware that they have a hard task before them. To truly gain from any magical efforts it is necessary to continually refine and redefine one's character – a hard road and one which appears to go on for ever. If a willing (and total) commitment to magic is not made then the individual will undoubtedly fail in his ambitions.

Magic is a calling that offers few rewards, mainly because any glory in the occult world is, by definition, hidden. Magic attracts those who were destined to be part of its ways from the beginning, and deters those who should not be involved. Those who would be foolish enough to 'dabble' in its ways are the last thing magic needs.

The old 'Schools of Magic' no longer exist, which is a great handicap for the genuine student. Arcane knowledge is now freely available to all, but that is no substitute for sound instruction. Wisdom does not automatically follow in the wake of a great deal of information, no matter how comprehensive. Neither will any student learn to be a magician from reading books – even this one! As in everything, 'practice maketh perfect', although there is no such thing as a perfect magician.

Magic has certainly enhanced my own life. It has brought me into the company of wise and wonderful people. I have gained more than a glimpse of wonders I did not know existed, and it has determined how I should live my life. It saw me through dark times and, when I returned to the light a wiser man, it brought me ineffable joy as a reward. If I am able to share some measure of the Inner Light, then I have to some degree repaid Isis, the Goddess I serve.

Gordon Strong
March 2011

Ruthlessness is the first principle of sorcery.

Carlos Castaneda

The universe is full of magical things patiently waiting for our wits to grow sharper.

Eden Philpotts

...Magic as black as Merlin could make it, and the whole sea was green fire and white foam with singing mermaids in it. And the Horses of the Hills picked their way from one wave to another by the lightning flashes! That was how it was in the old days!

Rudyard Kipling

How Magic Works

A magician is what he believes himself to be; a magician is where he believes himself to be.

Col. C.R.F. Seymour

Modern man appears to expend a lot of energy in a frantic search to discover some meaning in his existence. For some, ancient ways speak more strongly at this moment than at any other time in the last millennium. Was it so fantastic for visionaries to have spoken of a 'golden age' when all nature was undefiled and sacred, when a powerful spirit moved through and over all?

Magic in those far off days was simply something that happened. It was the role of the magician to reassure those of his tribe that the gods continued to acknowledge their existence. If certain things were needed for survival – rain for the crops, animals to hunt, fertility, healing – then the magician would have to provide them. Naturally, he had to be successful in his magical endeavours or his tenure would abruptly cease. More than a few redundant wizards may well have been exiled and consigned to a life of muttering to themselves in distant caves.

It is now supposed that an 'Iberian' religious tradition was in existence before the Egyptian culture. This indicates that there may have been an active spiritual consciousness that predates the era that is marked by the construction of megalithic monuments in the West. It is speculated that during early 'rituals' a desire to communicate with, honour (and probably placate) *earth spirits* was paramount. These spirits were not autonomous; they drew their power from above, and were the gods that are named in various different traditions – Thoth, Odin and Zeus.

The word *Magus* is the singular form of *Magi*, a title that once had the same distinction as a *Brahman* in India, or was inherent in the status of a Zoroastrian priest.[1] Among the Jews it was the task of the Magi to interpret passages of scripture and search for their inner meaning. In Egypt and Chaldea, the role of the Magus was as a diviner or a seer.

Never owning an orthodox role in society, and thus always outsiders, magicians were still regarded as having an authority. They held a rank above the common citizen, but, they did not always own a good reputation. The most infamous magician, in the view of Early Christians, was Simon Magus.[2] In the annals of the Western Magical Tradition, few have earned the title of Magus. Peuckert defines the calling as,

> ...one who follows the light of nature ... the magus used the light of nature to read the 'signatures' of the macrocosm in the microcosm...[3]

Polarity within deities – Apollo, Ra and Lugh – and their counterparts – Persephone Isis and Brigid – appeared during a later era. This pairing of male and female – god and goddess, priest and priestess is a fundamental principle of magic.

From the end of the Arthurian/Celtic times onward, magic began to walk a shadowy path. When Isis and Osiris, and the rest of the 'pagan' deities that followed, had been thoroughly reviled by the Christian Church, a new religious authority became established in the West. A secular power base from 1000 AD onwards, the Church would not tolerate the slightest trace of the old ways. As a result, the magician became even more an outcast – reviled, and frequently persecuted.

> The sorcerer of the Middle Ages (who) was usually squalid and necessitous; hence he coveted treasures: he was usually despised, and hence he longed for mastery, for the prestige of mystery amid the power of the strange arts: he was usually lonely and libidinous, and sought, by means of spells and philters, to compel the desires of women. To be rich

---

1 4000 BC.
2 Simon was 'the worker of magic' and founder of Gnosticism. Once the court magician of Nero, he was skilled in levitation and psychokinesis. He was demonised by the Apostles, particularly St.Paul, even though he was a practising Christian himself.
3 G. MacDonald Ross, *Occultism and Philosophy in the Seventeenth Century*. Lecture given at The Royal Institute of Philosophy 1983.

in worldly goods, to trample on one's enemies and to gratify the desires of the flesh – such are the ends, variously qualified and variously attained, of most Ceremonial magic.[4]

The spells listed in medieval grimoires, the only existing repository for that era's magic, are mostly a hotchpotch of repressed desires for wealth, sex and revenge. Thankfully, these incantations rarely work. With the Renaissance came a new vision, largely exploratory and rational – magic was consigned to the shadows of the past.

In England, the Dissolution of the Monasteries had the effect of ensuring that the secular would now always triumph over the spiritual. Henry VIII, England's most odious monarch, successfully removed any vestige of the transcendental from English Christianity. England, or more precisely Great Britain, had always embraced a singular kind of Catholicism from the beginning, one that differed greatly from that of Europe. The Synod of Whitby in 664 AD attempted to unify tenet and practice in the Church, but probably did not have as much influence as has been previously assumed by historians. Ireland, annexed from Rome geographically and certainly in temperament, carried on in its own merry way for the next three centuries.

For the English peasant, miracle plays – dramatisations of the Christian message from the Virgin birth to the resurrection – were tremendously popular. More ambitious productions, depicting angels, devils and illustrations of vice and virtue, followed. All seems to have been a dress-rehearsal for the highly orchestrated celebration of Mass.

Conducted by gloriously costumed dignitaries, amid clouds of pungent incense, in an imposing space decorated with colourful pennants – a grandiose spectacle it must have been. Not that the congregation actually engaged with the subtleties of the liturgy; apparently most of them wandered about the nave in a state of blissed-out ignorance.

Come the Reformation, countless works of art – many of staggering beauty – were destroyed. Places of worship that had displayed them were often trashed. The Anglican Church must be condemned – and is also much the poorer – for such an unforgiveable act of vandalism. The popular notion of worship – one that contained an aura of magic and mystery (even superstition), disappeared in this Protestant onslaught.

---

4   Arthur Versluis, *The Philosophy of Magic* (London: Routledge and Kegan Paul, 1986) p.112

The Tudors had ensured that the Holy Spirit would no longer flow from the Sacred Vessel. From then on it would be so filled with doctrinal dust as to be permanently dry.

A visit to Chartres cathedral, where Mass has even now the air of a magical ceremony, will enlighten those who wish to experience the power of old Christianity combined with a pre-Christian ambiance. Before parts of it became a New Age Disneyland, the town of Glastonbury in England was the same. The Abbey, the Holy Thorn, set against a backdrop of pagan vibrations from the Tor; all manifested the same dual force.

The New Age, with its eclecticism and miasma of illusions, has inevitably spawned both the prophet and the charlatan. Science, through cosmology and quantum physics has encouraged the philosophical mind to expand and explore new territory. Metaphysics, in an alliance which would once have been inconceivable, has joined with science in speculating upon the nature and workings of the cosmos.

Still, there are a majority who will only embrace a materialist 'reason', one fuelled by a media-inspired view of the world. The energy expended in denying the existence of magic by such dullards could be so easily used to promote such a wondrous instrument of harmony. Given that such prejudice against magic still exists, I would not advise practitioners to indulge in too much loose talk about magical practices. Even though, in our enlightened Western civilization an individual cannot be executed for his beliefs, he may still be ostracized.

Unless the individual is a determined materialist, a dimension of the mysterious or unexplained must have a place in anyone's personal philosophy. As Jung maintained throughout his life, '...our image of the world corresponds to reality only when the improbable has its place in it.'[5] No one knows anything for certain; the spiritual path simply guides the seeker in the direction of wisdom, or hopefully a greater understanding. Religion professes to achieve the same ends but with dogma taking the place of debate.

It is wise to remember that we have only a temporary tenure on this planet. With a shake of her tresses, Mother Earth can signal the end for us all. We should dedicate our time upon Earth to discovering how best to work in harmony with her. The true practitioner of magic does just that, and *only that* – as we shall discover. It is not man but the Divine

---

5   Gerhard Wehr, *Jung – A Biography* (Boston: Shambhala, 2001) p.68

Plan that determines whether anything undertaken will ever succeed. Human will has achieved extraordinary feats, but ultimately the divine impetus that brought the universe into existence will determine how it is shaped and how (and if) it will continue.

Magic is eternal; it is not restrained by the parameters of time or space. It is only the limitation of our senses or, as Wittgenstein might insist, *language*, that prevents us from achieving anything that we wish. The magician knows he may travel anywhere, see anything or do anything. Those in the Aquarian Age[6] will doubtless experience travel in other dimensions become commonplace – magicians have been doing this for centuries!

To cite a simple example of magical perception, suppose that we define lead as having the physical property of being 'heavy' – it is surely capable of being as light as a feather *if the magician so wishes*. Einstein bears this out when he states that, 'mass is a form of energy and can be converted into other forms of energy'.[7] In the same way, consciousness may be altered by means of 'magical forces'. Magic takes into account that all perception is by nature subjective, and thus it may be changed in accordance with the magician's will.

The manifestation of 'reality' is at the whim of creation. The madman or the drug-taker may be convinced that the world is peopled by purple monsters; the sober and sane insist these things do not exist. Sobriety does not necessarily guarantee a monopoly on perception. It is all a matter of what one *chooses* to see. The magician may also choose what is not seen. Aleister Crowley insisted that the secret of invisibility is,

> 'to prevent people noticing you when they would normally do so … I was able to take a walk in the street in a golden crown and a scarlet robe without attracting attention.'[8]

To the practitioner with a little experience, Crowley's words seem almost obvious. The key is that ordinarily we project our presence in order to be noticed, for whatever reason – maybe we wish to catch the

---

6   Minkowski, writing in 1909, suggested that 'Henceforth space by itself, and time by itself, are doomed to fade away into mere shadows, and only a kind of union of the two will preserve an independent reality.'

7   Bruce Rosenblum and Fred Kuttner, *Quantum Enigma Physics Encounters Consciousness* (London: Duckworth, 2006) p.48

8   Aleister Crowley, *The Confessions* (London: Penguin Arkana, 1987)

attention of a waiter in a restaurant, for instance. To remain unnoticed or 'invisible', the subject retracts his presence and projects nothing, or even less than nothing!

It cannot be stated too many times that there is only one purpose of magic and that is to do good. If magic is undertaken with any other motive it is not true magic. Those who glibly talk of 'the left hand' or the 'right hand path', as if it was no more important than opting for red or white wine at a dinner party, are under a gross misapprehension. Motive is all, and Magic is a serious business, one not to be undertaken lightly. Those who attempt to use it for any base purpose always come unstuck. Such perversity is playing with fire, whether they be the fires of hell or not makes little difference – fire always consumes.

The initiate should also restrain himself from being tempted to judge others or any situation, as much as possible. This particularly applies during the early magical training, when he is at his most sensitive. To discriminate is wise, to condemn or even to over-praise, is not. To believe one has the right to decide the fate of another human being leads to wickedness. The time for the world to learn this lesson is long overdue.

The magicians of the Elizabethan era and the next few centuries – John Dee, Paracelsus and Cornelius Agrippa and others not so celebrated – began the tradition of combining study with magical practice. They were scholars as well as masters of the Inner Planes, thus they could debate knowledgeably with other contemporary thinkers. To study and understand the practice of magic is essential before embarking upon any practice. For anyone to perform magic *without* being aware of what he is dealing with is not only foolish, but downright dangerous.[9]

Meditation

The definition of magic most often quoted is 'the ability to use the will in altering consciousness'. It should be understood that the

---

9   The danger lies not in the rash or foolish approach, but one that is half-hearted or uncertain. How one approaches the game of cricket might illustrate this. The ball is hard and certainly capable of hurting a player, but if he attacks it with the intention of mastery the chances are it that it will not. The Magus never doubts that he can achieve his purpose. He may not always succeed; the ritual may not gain its end, but this is not the point, *intent* is what is important.

magical consciousness is something very far removed from 'ordinary' consciousness. The 'everyday mind' – making mundane observations and gaining superficial impressions – is of no use in the practice of magic. As Carlos Castaneda's sorcerer Don Juan attempts to explain to his pupil,

> The world doesn't yield to us directly; the description of the world stands in between. So, properly speaking, we are always one step removed and our experience of the world is always a recollection of the experience. We are perennially recollecting the instant that has just happened, just passed. We recollect, recollect, recollect.[10]

We constantly encounter a world of falsehood, one that uses convention and opinion to create a 'real world'. The advent of electronic media in our own age has made this countless times easier and the practice of doing so even more insidious. We must strive to be aware! Susan Greenfield identifies the neurological mechanisms that *prevent* us from enjoying greater perception. She stresses the existence of

> ...other connections that intercept this incoming stream of information, projecting it back down in the opposite direction to modify the way the incoming signal is relayed and thus how the world is perceived. We see the world in terms of what we have seen already.[11]

If he is fortunate the magician may have a physical space that is his temple. Even if he does not, he should develop his own *inner temple* so he may journey there whenever he wishes. This constructing in the unconscious a place both familiar and meaningful is the first exercise in developing the *magical imagination.*

The term 'imagination' is often used in a pejorative sense by those who wish to belittle an original or unconventional idea. 'It's all just in your imagination', is a classic put-down. Did they but know it these scoffers are correct, it is 'all in the imagination'! The Universal Mind 'lies at the heart of magic...not so much a means to an end as it is a means to a higher means.'[12]

---

10 Castaneda, Carlos *Tales of Power* (London: Hodder & Stoughton, 1975) p.89
11 Greenfield, Susan. A., *The private life of the brain* (London: Allen Lane, 2000) p.65
12 Versluis p.7

The psychologist might consider the fruits of the unconscious mind to be subjective and nothing more; the magician knows better. As Dion Fortune, once a practising psychologist herself, informs us,

> An image formed by the imagination is a reality from the point of view of psychology; it is quite true that is has no physical existence, but are we going to limit reality to that which is material? We shall be far out of our reckoning if we do, for mental images are potent things, and although they do not actually exist on the physical pane, they influence it far more than people suspect.[13]

Meditation is the gateway to magic as yoga is another. Both practices relax the body and encourage the brain to exercise different mental faculties. It is via meditation that awareness is nurtured and other planes of existence revealed to the student. The Imagination is not the same as Fancy – roving thoughts – it is a creative faculty, one used to make forms. A principle of Hermeticism is that an idea can be made manifest, and the key to gaining this art is the power of concentration. The ability to sustain concentration can be increased with various exercises and meditation is the most obvious one.

Connecting with and contacting the inner worlds is the purpose of such exercises. Building up an instantly summoned channel is an essential task for the student of magic. Remember that what an individual chooses to retain there determines not only the nature of that world, but what he experiences in the mundane also. What you see is what you get! Or, as Aristotle said, more profoundly, 'The soul never thinks without images'. Also, as Gareth Knight informs us, 'the worlds available through the higher use of the imagination are every bit as real as the physical world.'[14]

The student should seek constantly to empower the inner mind. 'Day dreaming' is to be discouraged, for it encourages empty fantasies. Awareness of everything that is being perceived on both *the inner and outer planes* is essential, so that lessons may be learned. It could be said that the most valuable initiation takes place in silence. Crowley has this to say concerning how the magician should conduct himself:

---

13 Fortune, Dion, *Applied Magic and Aspects of Occultism* (London: HarperCollins, 1987)

14 Knight, Gareth, *Magical Images and the Magical Imagination* (Sun Chalice, 1998)

...every act is done noiselessly; all disturbance means clumsiness or blundering. The soldier may happen not to be hit as he carries his wounded comrade through the barrage, but there is no luck in magic. We work in a fluid world, where every moment is compensated at once.[15]

Great magical gain resides in the *retaining of images*. They have the same function as *keywords*, namely in setting up a resonance on the Inner Planes. If a meditation is begun by focusing on a particular symbol, one that has a strong relevance to the journey about to take place, then making the transition between worlds is made that much smoother. With all magical practice, the more the symbol is observed, and always with the same positive intent, then the quicker it becomes part of the *magical personality*.

The Practice of Meditation

Meditation is not an easy skill to acquire. At first the mind will resist the student's desire to control it. Perseverance is the key, and a regular time for the practice of meditation certainly aids in acquiring the skill. Dion Fortune suggests that the most efficacious time is upon waking. The establishing of a routine of time and place always helps, as will a consistently invoked image. The brain gradually gets accustomed to what is expected from it. Choose a comfortable (but not too comfortable) chair, close the eyes and concentrate on the prepared image. In Buddhist mediation the eyes are kept open, but this may be a technique not easy for the beginner to accomplish.

Thoughts will enter the consciousness unbidden. The beginner should not be over concerned by this. Simply observe the idea appear and then leave, before returning to the original state of concentration. The chosen image will gradually grow stronger and more potent. It will eventually become a thought form, and not only that, will be attached to an aura and thus create its own presence. Eventually it will be possible to summon this image at any time during the day or night. Dion Fortune speaks of 'a storage battery of spiritual force'[16] that acts 'as a mentor(s) during periods of spiritual dryness'.

---

15 Crowley, *ibid.*, p.279
16 Fortune, *ibid.*, p.137

Some practitioners find incense, or a burning candle an aid to concentration, it is all a matter of personal preference. Dion Fortune goes so far as recommending the initiate to wear a 'meditation robe' of thin black silk. Any aids that make the meditation successful can only be of benefit. The goal is to experience being conscious and unconscious at the same time. As Christine Hartley informs us,

> You must withdraw consciously from the world around you without losing consciousness. Gradually you still your roving thoughts, your active mental brain; you refuse to admit the sounds you hear, not by sending them away from you but by withdrawing from them, and gradually you will be able to see yourself standing within the envelope of your body but able to leave it with your mind.[17]

Some occultists warn of the danger inherent in putting too much store upon the random images that appear during meditation. This is a valid point, for these 'visions' are considered always to be subjective and, although often diverting, are of little value to the student's magical progress.

Symbols

Goethe describes a symbol as 'a living momentary revelation of the inscrutable'. Symbols are the first recorded attempts at a visual depiction of a significant concept. All ancient cultures possess them and often these simple marks and drawings are intrinsically similar. The square, circle and triangle seem to have been the first figures that represented basic concepts, respectively the earth, the sun, and the heavens.

W.G.Gray, as always, is most helpful on the subject.

> The whole of Occultism and Magic is full of Symbols which are absolutely crammed with compressed energies and connected straight to direct supply-lines leading to undreamed of reservoirs of consciousness. Once we discover how to turn the keys, an Infinity of Intelligence awaits us. This is why the art of Ceremonial Symbolism is so valuable. It teaches us how to manipulate Meanings in relation to Manifestations, and to work Will with Word.[18]

---

17 Alan Richardson, *Dancers to the Gods: The Magical Records of Charles Seymour and Christine Hartley 1937-1939* (Wellingborough: Aquarian Press, 1985) p.67
18 W.G.Gray, *Magical Ritual Methods* (Cheltenham: Helios Book Service, 1969) p.123

The contemplation of symbols, and the systematic absorbing of them into the inner consciousness, is the next stage in training the magical mind. The realization of their immense power only occurs when they are truly part of us. As has already been stated, we must learn to invoke certain images at any given moment. Our meditation practice should make acquiring this technique much easier. Focus is the key, and if the association is embraced in detail and wholeheartedly the relevant image will automatically appear in the inner mind.

As Gareth Knight explains:

> ... (those) that we wish to designate magical images are those that do not merely 'represent' something else. A magical image resonates to a higher kind of reality. It carries within itself something that is 'not of this world'[19]

The ability to sustain an idea can be trained with various mental exercises.[20] It saves so much time and trouble if the magician has a sign, password or image that he can use for instant contact with the kingdom that lies beyond the veil. A symbol distills the details of an idea into one easily assimilated 'spirit seed'. The images of the Tarot are an excellent example; they are an illustrated book that depicts every mode of human consciousness.

For an image to remain permanently in the inner consciousness, it must have credence in the life of the initiate. This is where the intellectual and the intuitive meet, without either one ousting its so-called rival. The developed mind should always strive to achieve a balance between reason and intuition.

The skill is such that the student learns to contemplate an object deeply enough to discover its intrinsic qualities. For instance, a meditation upon 'the cup' should go far beyond just experiencing the physical object, and release its inner meaning. Transferring to the inner being what 'the cup' has represented in history and in myth is just a beginning. The next stage would be experiencing the vital energy that such an artefact owns.

No symbol may be regarded in isolation. For instance, if the cup is being studied, it should be regarded in relation to the lance, and how the two qualities (the elements of water and air, female and male)

---

19 Knight, *ibid.*, p.11
20 Mounhi Sadhu, *Concentration* (London: Allen and Unwin 1963).

interact. The purpose of this exercise, as any magical study, is to gain the greatest understanding through the *breadth* of one's vision; that is, seeing all possibilities.

We should not consider that these ideas are somehow exclusive to our age. Coleridge once posited that there existed a *Secondary Imagination*, which he described as,

> ...a higher or deeper level of consciousness, that can create with the images of the mind ... and communicate at a profound level...[21]

The poet is describing the ability to interpret impressions that come to us from the higher worlds, these operating through the agency of symbols. Ignatius Loyola, the founder of the Jesuit order, developed certain spiritual exercises which he termed 'Simple Contemplation'. The technique was to include oneself in a particular scene (in his method, episodes from the New Testament) to the extent that the imagined scenario and the individual merged into one.

It is important to realize that the magical imagination is a creative tool. It is the Universal Mind that 'lies at the heart of magic...not so much a means to an end as it is a means to a higher means.'[22] The mechanics of perception are of interest to the occultist only as far as they may help him to develop and refine his powers. It is important to realise that the *mind* is different to the *brain*. The brain is an organ like any other in the body and functions perfectly well unless physically damaged. The 'mind' is the term we give to the phenomenon of experiencing consciousness. By understanding the way the brain works, we realise that a 'magical perception' is of a very different order to other ways that incoming information is interpreted. Susan Greenfield again provides us with a valuable insight, when she asks us to:

> ...imagine that a replica of yourself could be built from transported data downloaded from your brain. However, a sad consequence of doing so would be that the original cells would be killed; on the bright side, they would be reconstructed again in exact replication. Your replica would be effectively you, because he or she would have inherited your brain, along with all its memories. The replica would think that it had been you all the time, when really it may only have been so for a trice. [23]

---

21 Gareth Knight, *A History of White Magic* (London: Mowbrays, 1978), p.5.
22 Versluis, *ibid.*, p.7
23 Greenfield, *ibid.*, p. 27.

All of which confirms that a purely *intellectual* approach, one that excludes unpredictable or visionary notions, can only be capable of producing a very limited view of existence. Research in the same field by philosopher Dan Dennett suggests that,

> '...at any one moment there is a salient brain state, amounting to a complex consciousness, that is highly transient, just one of many different drafts of one's take on the world ... people conflate learning – a behavioural change – with understanding – an inner process.'[24]

This proposal, using an academic parlance, seeks to explain the difference between *Wisdom* and *Understanding*, a vital element of 'understanding' in itself. Now that we know the means to contact the Inner Planes, we must realise that this is only the beginning. It is important that the student has a precise idea of what it is that he strives for in these exercises and ultimately in the practice of magic itself.

Astral Projection

Samadhi is the Eastern term for 'higher trance', a state brought about when the physical self is deliberately left behind. The super-consciousness and the subconscious are then linked so that images are created to illustrate that which exists on other planes. An example of this is the manifestation of etheric double referred to by the Ancient Egyptians as *Ka*. The priestly class were all too aware of the possibility of 'astral flight'. It is possible for the student to peruse an invocation, depicted in hieroglyphs.[25]

The ancients were all too aware that the soul, when liberated from the restrictions of its physical shell, could travel over incredible distances. To demonstrate this, the Lamas of Tibet communicated with each other over many hundreds of miles by causing the astral body to manifest itself in another place. A method of liberating the spirit from the body may also be found in *The Tibetan Book of the Dead*. Although intended for ensuring the entry of the soul into clear light at the moment of death, much that is written of the process is relevant to our study.

---

24 Greenfield, *ibid.,* pp.28-30.
25 Alan Richardson, *The Magician's Tables: A Complete Book of Correspondences* (London: Godsfield Press, 2007)

In order to achieve astral projection a certain state of mind and body is required. Physical well-being does not necessarily aid astral projection, but it will greatly strengthen the spirit. Those who regularly practise meditation will already have experience of a transcendental state. It is essential that the mind be fully focused during these endeavours, for it is not possible to achieve astral projection solely with the will. Will, *plus* the imagination, does the trick. More specifically, the *passive will* should be brought into play. *Not* making an effort, *not* doing, *not* trying – is the way.

The spirit is most responsive during the fourteen days between the advent of the new moon and her waxing to the full. The student should seek to encourage the release of the astral body by attempting certain exercises. Reflecting upon projection before sleep is one preparation, as dreams of projection should follow. The dream state is a springboard for projection. *Lucid dreaming* is a valuable asset for much spiritual work. If at any time while dreaming an awareness of experiencing the feeling of being inside the dream occurs, then any of the following actions should be attempted:

1. Reading a book
2. Flying
3. Turning on a light switch
4. Looking in a mirror

The deliberation required to perform any of these acts profoundly affects the nature of the dreaming process and enables the dreamer to gain control of the dream. In this way the dreamer may determine events within the dream, and this gives the student who would attempt projection a distinct advantage.

Around midnight is an excellent time to perform astral projection as the universe is at its most still at this moment. The astral body is released from the region of the solar plexus; thus laying upon one's back aids the release. This position also makes the return easier. Those who practise Yoga will be familiar with the techniques of abdominal breathing. This exercise automatically relaxes the solar plexus centre.

The actual release of the astral body is achieved by passing from the dream state to the astral state. Prepare for normal sleep and, while doing so, imagine climbing a set of stairs. As the topmost step is reached the astral body should be willed to fly into the void. A cry or grunt may be emitted at this point! Like all occult techniques this requires practice, and there may be a return to consciousness, or instead a sliding into the dream state.

Three different types of projection may be experienced. *Levitation* is the sensation of flying over a landscape that has strange or unfamiliar features. *Gliding* is travelling towards a destination where *en route* familiar landmarks may be seen. *Skrying* is the sensation of moving upwards to heaven. The Buddhists maintain that angels appear in great numbers during skrying and it is possible to arrive at the gates of heaven and experience a mortal 'death'. Apparently, rejuvenation of the body is supposed to take place during skrying.

If the astral traveller wishes to arrive at a particular earthly location during projection, it is essential to visit the place beforehand and make oneself familiar with as many of its physical details as possible. Before projection, focusing strongly on the intended destination is essential. The subsequent arrival may be instantaneous, or impressions of the journey (including landmarks known to the traveller) may be experienced on the way. It is also possible for the traveller to be visible to another person during a projection. If this is done as a deliberately pre-arranged exercise it will have more chance of success if the seer has an affinity with the host.

Unconscious projection is a phenomenon that happens to the regular traveller when *dreams of projection* turn into actual projection. In this instance, the astral body hovers above the physical body at such close proximity that the astral body may desire to suddenly 'return home'. If this occurs the experience is often accompanied by a severe jolt, enough even to cause the body to twist and turn convulsively.

Magical Contacts

By means of ritual, and the regular practice of meditation, higher beings may be encountered upon the Inner Planes. It is relevant here to mention the astral journeys made by Colonel Seymour and Christine Hartley that took place in the 1930s. In the quotation that follows, '2QT' refers to Number Two, Queensborough Terrace, the building where Dion Fortune supervised her magical school.

The *modus operandi* of their work was simple. Wearing their voluminous cloaks to shut out worldly influences they sat down on two chairs before the gas fire in 2QT, held hands, closed eyes, and projected their consciousness beyond the pylon gates into the Otherworld.[26]

The student would be well-advised to study the complete accounts as they demonstrate very dramatically what may be achieved during astral practice.

It must be stressed that what occurs in a genuine astral contact is rarely a random procession of events. In the student's case, images of a particular figure will permeate the conscious mind some time before the actual meeting. Dion Fortune herself speaks of a period of three years' work before she was actually 'received' by her own contact. Whatever the images that the student receives, the effort should be taken to fix these in the mind. Study the antecedents or historical period from where the potential contact springs. Psychic work alone is not enough in this situation, a solid foundation of research is absolutely necessary to make real progress.

When it is considered that the correct moment has arrived, the face and form of the contact desired should be visualized. If the student owns an actual image of the contact then he can use a technique that is often used to train the inner vision. The image is contemplated for some period and then the gaze is transferred to a blank wall where it will appear. The next stage is to 'log' it into the inner mind; the unconscious should record it in sufficient detail that it may be recalled at will.

Naturally, it must be established in some way that the contact sought is willing to participate in the exercise. It is a case of *suitability* for the initiate. Like attracts like in every sphere, and a situation very similar to romantic love is often apparent between an initiate and the contact. A melding of two auras may take place, something very akin to the total absorption in each other that lovers experience. The relationship of an artist and his muse is similar. The Priest and Priestess conducting a magical ceremony would be only too familiar with this kind of symbiosis.

The actual moment when the contact is made is often accompanied by a sudden charge of energy. Such a phenomenon is often experienced at particular moments during a ritual. The contact may impart

---

26 Richardson, *ibid.,* p.78

information that is valuable to the seeker (in the same way that spirits at sacred sites have this power) but it must be acknowledged that only a small percentage of the information received from Inner Plane contacts is of value.

The student should respect his contacts but not be cowed or intimidated by them. Those who stand before the gods are gods themselves. Hence the advice of Dion Fortune, to *believe that you are the god you seek*. In the times when spirit walked, Man created gods in his own way and we have inherited the power to evoke them once again if we wish.

The student will gain even more knowledge of these matters if he seeks out a teacher. The Masters of the Inner Planes pass on their secrets to magical practitioners who in turn teach this wisdom to others. Much of this teaching is done unconsciously, and the most valuable lessons are learned this way. Reflect upon the time you have spent in the company of a wise magus. You will realize that not much might have been actually said, but a great deal has been *unconsciously* passed on to you.

2

Divination

...the untrained man is very apt to think that he is the helpless victim of fate. Did the revelations of astrology stimulate him to greater efforts, they would serve a useful purpose, but how often is this the case? How much oftener do we see their findings used as an excuse for laissez-faire?

Dion Fortune

The practice of interpreting what appears to be a random combination of phenomena as being a reflection of an individual's past, present, or future life is very ancient. Country sayings, usually applied to the behaviour of birds and still to be heard, are a Celtic tradition.[27] Acknowledging that everything in the physical world is connected – so we may learn wisdom from all creatures as well as the living Earth – is a basic principle of magic. In an urban environment, where the natural world has been subdued or eradicated, to achieve a strong connection with Gaia is difficult, if not almost impossible. These days the magician must rely on nurturing his Inner World and reconnecting with these eternal, natural forces when he travels to that kingdom.

All manner of means are employed to 'predict the future', many being extremely spurious. The accuracy of the insights received depends entirely upon the aptitude and talent of the medium. It is almost impossible to 'become' a medium. Any training for that purpose, once in the hands of Romanies and their ilk, has degenerated into a commercial practice of most dubious worth.

---

27 The Tibetans have for millennia embraced the notion that sighting cranes, geese, ducks and swans was auspicious, to the point of the observer receiving the Buddha's blessing when this occurred.

The magician does not concern himself with 'fortune telling', though he should have a thorough knowledge of the mysteries, as Dion Fortune explains.

> The Tree of Life, astrology and the tarot are not three mystical systems, but three aspects of one and the same system, and each is unintelligible without the other. [28]

The initiates of the Golden Dawn were made to diligently study these disciplines in their initial studies in the First Order, so that they would have a familiarity with ancient principles. The Qabalah in particular has its own idiosyncratic wisdom as we shall discover.

A basic error is ever to *assume* anything about the world. This is tantamount to being *unaware*, and if the student of magic continues in this manner for any length of time he is courting great danger. A situation should be evaluated *intuitively* as well as with reference to previous experience. To express this as a simple formula, it may well be that on A+B = C on Monday, yet Tuesday's situation might be closer to A+B = Z.

Psychism too is of little value if it is not controlled. One of the shortcomings of the New Age is that being 'in touch' with mystical experiences is considered to be an end in itself. 'Insights' gained by the amateur or inexperienced medium are generally worthless. Discipline, study and common sense are the basic ingredients for this kind of work, *as well as* 'insights'. Those who believe that they can become an astrologer or a Tarot reader by enrolling in a weekend course are deluding themselves.

Astrology and Numerology

Western Astrology (Greek *astros,* star), as opposed to Vedic[29] astrology, originated in Babylonia and spread to Greece. A theoretical system of interpreting the influence of the planets on human behaviour, the horoscope (Greek *horoskopos*) shows the position of the planets at a

---

28 Dion Fortune, *The Mystical Qabalah* (New York, USA: Ibis, 1981) p. 73
29 Unlike Western Astrology (which has much to do with Egyptian decanic astrology – from where it probably originated) Vedic Astrology refers to the actual procession of the equinoxes.

particular time and place. From this 'map' the astrologer suggests certain tendencies, strengths and weaknesses in any situation, this practice being known as *horary astrology*. The Hermeticists and Neo-Platonic philosophers adapted the Babylonian system to incorporate genethiliacal astrology – the 'birth chart' as we know it – the earliest example dating from 410 BC.

The interaction between the sidereal zodiac and the local horizon provides the frame of reference for interpretation, and the angular aspects between the planets are a further aid. The horoscope is also divided into twelve celestial houses, each one governing a feature of human affairs. The planets that occupy these houses suggest to the astrologer the potential for success, or the presence of shortcomings in particular areas of the native's life or character. Predictive astrology is concerned with applying 'transits' and 'progressions' to ascertain the effect of future planetary activity on the natal horoscope.

The key to the mechanics of astrology is an understanding of the notion of *triplicities* and *quadruplicities*. The former represents the division between signs of the zodiac that are fixed (unmoving, established) cardinal (active, potent) and mutable (adaptive, changing). The latter deals with the four elements – fire, air, earth and water. A combination of these two groupings defines a zodiacal sign i.e. Aries – Cardinal/Fire.

The *degree* of energy, combined with the nature of that energy, always manifests in the physical world in an observable manner. The student would do well to reflect upon the artist's adage that 'tone is more important than colour.' The elements harmonise or are discordant – to produce a reaction. It is also as well to realise that without a certain amount of friction nothing is achieved. Too much conflict, however, results in a state of near permanent tension. When the astrologer talks of 'difficult aspects' it is to this situation that he refers.

With technology enabling the astrologer to instantly plot a nativity, progressions and the rest, the tendency has been in the last twenty or so years for the practice of astrology to become more quantitative than qualitative. The design of a medieval nativity would be incomprehensible to the modern astrologer, yet the insights gained by his Dark Age counterpart would have been just as great, if not greater. The danger of the modern approach is that the intuitive faculty is lost and astrology then ceases to be a demonstration of *morphic resonance* [30] – each part of the cosmos reflecting another, and becomes a 'ticking boxes' exercise.

As an aid to the student's own magical development, astrology may be extremely valuable. To understand why particular antipathy or attraction exists in our nature, and how they may be resolved, is an obvious advantage. We should not however ignore that celebrated Latin tag, *Astra inclinant, non necessitant* – 'The stars incline, they do not compel'.

Intrinsic to the fabric of astrology is *numerology* – the significance of number. *Omnia in mensura et numero et pondere disposuisti* – a phrase attributed to Sir Isaac Newton – 'God created everything by number, weight and measure' has a meaning greater than suggesting calculation has a divine origin. In medieval times 'arithmetic' was entirely different to our modern methods and still incorporated an element of which the Ancients were only too aware – that of the symbolic nature of numbers. Three was a trinity, four – security, five – of man etc. According to one authority:

> When the qualitative aspects are included in our conception of numbers, they become more than simple quantities 1, 2, 3, 4 etc. They acquire an archetypal character such as Unity, Opposition, Conjunction and Completion. They are then analogous to more familiar archetypes, such as the Mother, the Wise Old Man, the Maiden, and the Shadow... [31]

The practice of assigning a number to each letter of the alphabet probably followed the advent of writing.

Modern numerologists take the letters of an individual's name, plus the total obtained by the addition of the digits of the birthdate, and from this produce a key number. This designates the number assigned to an individual's life path, and from this information various indications of character and events that are likely to take place are deduced.

---

30 'Is it not possible that a sudden gust of wind in Putney High Street markedly affects the prices of plums in Kowloon Market, Putney High Street?' The anonymous but lyrical sentiment that accompanies this thesis.

31 Llewellyn, *Pythagorean Numerology* (St.Paul, Minnesota: Llewellyn International 2001) p.68

Sun and Moon

The esoteric relationship between the Sun and the Moon is undeniably significant. In occultism the Sun has, as its progenitor, a greater sun – one that is 'behind' it, and the epitome of all light and creation. Of its partner, the Moon, Dion Fortune has this to say:

> Our Lady is also called the Moon, called of some Selene, of others Luna, but by the wise Levanah, for therein is contained the number of her name. She is the ruler of the tides of flux and reflux. The waters of the Great Sea answer unto her; likewise the waters of all earthly seas, and she ruleth the nature of women.[32]

The nature of the otherworld – the *Inner Mind* – is represented by the Moon reflecting the conscious awareness of the Sun. They are as brother and sister, and providing a certain stability for each other.

Contemplating an image of the Holy Grail may be helpful in comprehending this relationship. The *Shekinah* is the dwelling place of the Sun's light. In the centre of the Sun is its soul – the divine understanding – which is the essence of the Grail. Conversely, when the Moon – as the Cup – contains the Sun, what is within is the light of inspiration. It is said that the Grail is 'empty yet it is full' – its content being the invisible light.

The magician celebrates the seasons. He also pays particular attention to the phases of the moon, the tendency for expansion when it is waxing, and also the nature of the waning Moon to contract or limit. He is also aware of how the Full Moon will radiate energy dependent upon the astrological sign that it occupies. A full moon in Leo will generate a very different vibration from one which occupies the sign of Scorpio. The lunar vibration affects the unconscious behaviour of humanity more than anyone could possibly realise. As Nietzsche maintained, '...the greatest part of conscious thought must still be attributed to [non-conscious] instinctive activity.'

The Moon is one of the forces that is responsible for our well-being, because it controls the emotions. We must all learn to control our feelings – that is the challenge. To be insensitive implies a lack of awareness, but as always a balance exists – the magician must never be

---

32 Fortune, *ibid.*, p.131

slave to his emotions. 'Passion is the enemy of wit', is a saying that is most relevant as it implies that extreme feeling throws the self into a disordered state, one near to chaos. An excess of emotion may also be debilitating, causing weariness, a weakening of the will, and leaving an overwhelming helplessness in its wake. Order is inherent in magic, reflected in the pattern of ritual – sober, deliberate and demonstrating logical form. The practical and the pragmatic are still the essence of magical practice.

The Tarot

The Tarot is a book of philosophy, an amalgam of archetypes and images that has the power to illustrate any human situation. Its history is convoluted, as are all occult artefacts, and many different claims have been made as to its origins. It is doubtful whether it has existed in its present form any longer than that of ordinary playing cards, i.e. since the 14th century. As a source of wisdom it is invaluable, as an aid to magical practice its potency is self-evident. The sometimes vexed question of its use as a method of divination will be discussed later.

I have written extensively upon the Tarot[33] and devoted a great part of my life to working with its powers. All of its secrets can never be known, and that is as it should be. Its potential as a means of illumination never ceases to impress me and will always do so. The benefit that the magician may gain from the Tarot depends entirely upon the amount of effort that he is prepared to put into studying it, and more important how much he engages with its inner essence.

The Tarot consists of seventy-eight cards; twenty-two of these are referred to as the Major Arcana, the remaining fifty-six as the Minor Arcana. The word 'Arcana' is defined as 'a mystery that may be solved'. That is the challenge and the value of the exercise. The Qabalah presents the same challenge to us, in that it invites us to make connections, and interpret what we see in an entirely different way. When this re-orientating of thinking begins to take place (perhaps prompted by study of the Tarot) then the aspiring magician will be in a better position to understand the real nature of magic.

---

33 Gordon Strong, *Tarot Unveiled* (London: Mutus Liber, 2009)

A fixed intellectual approach may serve well enough within academic disciplines, but in the metaphysical world it will meet with only a limited success. The Qabalah or the Tarot cannot be understood solely by employing reason – the student will need to acquire other skills. Neither can these two systems be mastered solely with intuition – that is not so either. The great value of the Tarot as a teacher is that it encourages, perhaps insists, that the thinking remains flexible. It is almost as if a new language must be learned, one that communicates fully with the symbols and images that make up the Tarot.

One approach to be strenuously avoided in any study of the Tarot is that of classifying individual cards as either 'good' or 'bad'. This is the dualistic approach, and dreary old duality is a substitute for incisive thought. This adherence to extremes became the deadweight of fundamentalism in religion. The belief that if an idea is not totally embraced then opposing it must be wrong, is anathema to any real perception or understanding. Resign this way of thinking to the mental scrap-heap where it belongs!

Notions of black and white, perhaps even male and female (as they so easily become stereotypical), must be put aside. Heaven and Hell are inventions of man, not the Cosmos. Neither state exists; therefore, as material for contemplation, both are worthless. The student should consider the following premise: God created the world, and in there is both good and evil, therefore God is equally good and evil.

As Heraclitus declared, 'To God all things are fair and good and right, but men hold some things wrong and some right.'[34] The rock of faith is accepting that what occurs is supposed to occur. How events affect the individual may not always be to their liking, but that is almost irrelevant. The magician must pass through periods of darkness as well as light – that is the nature of the path to enlightenment.

The Major Arcana

It is not within the scope of this work to describe all seventy-eight cards of the pack in detail, but what follows is a brief discussion of certain cards that appear to be relevant in a *magical context*.

---

34 Heraclitus, fragment 102

The Fool represents the magical energy. He stands between worlds, poised in the space that magic also occupies. The Fool wants for nothing except the ability to choose, and therein lies his power – that of being able to perceive anything and everything and from all angles. This Arcanum also symbolises the realization that 'all is possible', as it is in any humorous view of the world, and is an aspect of The Fool in his 'foolery'.

The Magician is akin to the scientist in that he is detached emotionally. He is also a philosopher and a psychologist, like Jung, a figure who revealed,

> …I am a solitary, because I know things and must hint at things which other people do not know, and usually do not even want to know.[35]

The magus transforms the power that the Fool owns, and manifests it in whatever way he wishes. The 'neutral' aspect of the magician, in that he is a medium for power beyond himself, confirms another magical principle. Terms as 'white' or 'black' have no validity in magic, it is the purpose to which power is put that is significant and that is determined by the practitioner. If magic owns a colour at all, it is grey. 'Black magic' would appear to be magic without light, with an association of metaphorically groping around in the dark.

The High Priestess represents the polarity of magic, the interaction between Priest and Priestess. The seeker must know what lies beyond the veil in order to succeed in his quest. We must not resist change, for then our fears create a tension which will not allow energy to flow freely. The result is stagnation and sterility leading ultimately to death. If we always allow others to choose for us, the will is rendered powerless and our courage and tenacity disappear. By contacting this *goddess energy* we access the greatest guidance. The High Priestess is the symbol of purity and virginity – as Diana the huntress. [36]

Her light may be cold and fragile but it is *part of the darkness, not a rival to it*. In magical terms, the Magician *dares* whereas the High Priestess *knows*. The Fool and the Magician are both in action, while the High Priestess and the Empress are in repose. They have transformed

---

35 Wehr, *ibid.*, p. 22
36 And none may see the goddess naked, which is an allegory for 'that beyond the veil'. None may discover this, as Actaeon discovered, suffering a terrible fate for his impertinence.

the raw power of magic into something serene. Their concentration is as intense but it is has a different *modus operandi*. Neither the male nor the female must prevail one over the other, for a sense of equilibrium is at the heart of the Tarot.

The Empress is surrounded by fecundity and growth. Unlike the High Priestess she likes to *display* her beauty and munificence by bearing fruit and bestowing light and life. She is the natural world, the Earth at its most fertile and good – the spirit of Gaia. She also desires the sexual energy of the Emperor so that their union will bear fruit. Earth spirits reside in her kingdom, where trees and stones have an inner life and all is holy. She reminds us that the earthly realm has as much spirituality as the dominions of the other elements.

The number of the Empress is III – the *Trinity* – an acknowledgement of three states of being – mother, father and child. The Hindu triad has Vishnu the Preserver, Shiva the Destroyer and Brahmin the Absolute. No part of the trinity can exist without the other, thus sustaining an eternal state of change. In the Egyptian pantheon it is the trine of Isis, Osiris and Horus.

The Emperor represents the highest earthly power. He represents the power of *life* and holds the *Ankh*, the Egyptian symbol of vitality,[37] and yet, in his heart, The Emperor knows he owns only *temporal* power. Traditionally, a king holds the world (the orb) in one hand and the symbol of his power over it (the sceptre) in the other. By serving their king, his subjects imbue him with energy. It is to be hoped that this power is used well, for not every monarch possesses the virtue of *temperance*.

The Tarot Emperor is a man of reason, not easily swayed in his opinion and inclined to the coldest of logic. With him, there is little middle ground; his views are black and white. Not necessarily narrow-minded, but always single minded. He is the father, just and protective, but when his energy is misdirected he becomes the *tyrant*. The number of the Emperor is IV. It is the first number that can be factorized. It forms the square, which in turn becomes the cube. In this Arcanum structure is born. However, straight lines restrict and enclose – four is *rigid*. Its *limitations* are in its very weight and purpose.

---

37 The symbol of Isis, who is associated with the water sign of Cancer. A magical polarity, that of Fire and Water, exists here.

The Chariot is the other *lunar* card in the pack and the black and white images echo The High Priestess. *Emotion* is the motif of this Arcanum and more than that, the ability to control one's feelings – a necessity, and a sign of a stable character. Any rush of unrestrained emotion can be as destructive to the psyche as an avalanche or a flood in the physical domain. Cloying sentiment is as weakening as unbridled anger; either can overwhelm the senses and blind reason.

The Charioteer has a talent for creating illusions. He is the actor whose words move the crowd, the conjurer at whose tricks we marvel. So comfortable is he in his domain of mist and shadows that he sometimes fails to notice when others are lost or out of their depth. Even when they are drowning he may leave them to their fate. In his dark mood, he is as cold and lifeless as the moon. His character is essentially feminine, but it is not receptive like *The High Priestess* who rules the Temple. Do not be taken in by the glamour surrounding *The Chariot*, its wheels have the power to crush those who are foolish enough to stray into its path.

Death is the most valuable teacher we can have! The Buddhist says, 'Nothing exists, nothing has ever existed, nothing will ever exist.' meaning that no event which has ever occurred has made the slightest difference to the universe. Thus we might suggest that nothing anybody says or does has any significance either! Understand that and you will develop a love for the world as great as if you were personally its creator. The true artist knows that in *the act* is where the art lies not in the result. The end of a life means nothing to life itself. The sun still rises, the birds continue to sing, and the stars do not fall from the sky. Our own brief sojourn has ended, and that is all.

Life resides with the self, Death with the non-self. To regard Death as the agency of the divine is the beginning of wisdom. We may cheat death once, or even twice if we are very lucky, but he always wins in the end. Death, like The Magician, is distant from the affairs of men. Is the sun in the tarot card of Death rising or setting? It does not matter – time is an illusion. Better to regard existence as an endless series of changes than a tedious progress of the hours.

The Devil has an influence that cannot be ignored. No salvation exists in his domain; it is a place of barrenness and cynicism. No hope or joy resides there and the souls in bondage to the Devil remain empty and wretched. Temptation comes to us when our will is weak. We are constantly tested – the more so the closer we are to our spiritual goal.

We must trust the divine, for if once we deny that protection we are lost. The Devil desires us, like Faustus, to turn our back on the angels and think only of ourselves.

As the outsider and the outcast Lucifer is the *fallen angel*, which gives a more romantic cast to the picture. Blake wrote that 'The lust of the goat is the bounty of God.' and indeed *Pan* or *Cernunnos*, *The Lord of Animals* is the nature god. In this incarnation the Saturnine element seems altogether more attractive. He will frighten us when he leaps out of the wild wood but he is not *sinister*, simply a spirit of the earth. Priapic *Pan* is bursting with unbridled sexuality and taunts the prude and the puritan. The Church stigmatised the Pagan way, but ironically it is now a flourishing faith in its own right in The New Age.

The Reader

The interaction between the medium and the seeker of insights is a peculiar one. That is to say that in order for the 'message' to flow, the dynamics of the situation must be particularly finely balanced. Jung is discussing psychoanalysis here, but the point he makes is relevant to our subject.

> …the relationship between two people is built and worked out not only on the conscious level. On the one hand each of the two is in contact with his own unconscious, but on the other hand the unconscious of one acts upon and reacts to the unconscious of the other…[38]

It is arguable that the Tarot should not be used as a means of divination, as it is strictly speaking 'a book of philosophy'. It would be unreal to suggest that the Tarot is not used for divination, of course it is. The offer of 'readings' at psychic fairs has become almost an industry. It must also be said that there are 'readers' who do not have the scholarship, the ethics or, most important, the aptitude, to use the Tarot either wisely or well.

However, even fools and charlatans serve a purpose in this world. Who is not to say that nonsense has a value if it appears at the right moment and in the right context? The querent gets the reader he

---

38 Jung, *ibid.*, p.470

deserves, and if someone feels more at ease after a worthless reading, are we in a position to deny its benefit, even if it is only fleeting?

The genuinely mediumistic reader is most certainly performing a kind of magic, and one that is extremely powerful. Though as we have come to realise in our study, with power comes great responsibility, and one that should never be taken lightly. The true *seer*, one such as Edgar Cayce, was a rare individual. There is always the possibility of the medium passing on false information, even though their conviction and intention may be sincere. As Jung remarks,

> Every human judgment, however great one's subjective conviction might be, is subject to error, especially judgments which deal with transcendental subjects.[39]

The Tarot is a great teacher. It informs, and it will tell you anything you wish to know – or what you ought to know – eventually. Like all great teachers the cards know instinctively when any person is ready to receive a particular wisdom. We are constantly being given lessons and The Tarot is a distillation of that cosmic instruction. The Tarot is a *vision* of our world and the ongoing story of our lives; it does not exist outside the world, in a realm of make-believe.

On being a medium, Aleister Crowley remarked,

> One acquires what one may almost call a new sense. One feels in one's self whether one is right or not. The diviner must develop this sense.[40]

I would not seek to deter anyone who aspires to be a reader from their ambition. Equally I would make it plain to anyone who intends to read *professionally* that they must be absolutely certain of what they are doing, and even more important, why they are doing it. As always, motive is all. I make the same strictures with regard to those who would practise magic. These are deep waters, and being out of one's depth in the mystical tides can be extremely alarming indeed.

---

39 Jung, *ibid.*, p.476
40 Aleister Crowley, *Magic in Theory and Practice* (London: Penguin Arkana, 1987) p.271

3

The Qabalah

Each of the sefirot represented a different force or aspect of God,
such as love, power, or understanding.

Anon.

To the student confronted by the Qabalah[41] for the first time, much he encounters will be confusing. The terms are unfamiliar, the concepts seem impossibly complex, and the whole schema appears to be opaque. It would be the exceptional person who could, from the very beginning, understand its many levels of meaning. Perhaps that is as it should be, and that the wisdom of the Qabalah is revealed in a manner and at a pace suitable to the temperament of the individual student.

The word Qabalah means 'to receive' and is to be found within the *Zohar* – 'splendour' – a set of documents dating from the fourteenth century. The Qabalah[42] is supposedly the means that may be employed to utilise the magical treatise of Moses. Its origins may not be quite so straightforward. For Jewish scholars to claim exclusive rights to its content is somewhat disingenuous on their part.

Enough evidence exists to indicate that Moses learned the powers of magic during his sojourn in Egypt. Not only is this mentioned in the Bible,[43] E. Wallis Budge also details the miraculous act of transforming

---

41 The *Kabbalah* is the Judaic tradition; *Qabalah* is the mystical, and *Cabbala* the Christian.
42 The Qabalah within the Zohar is classified under the Practical, Literal, Unwritten and Dogmatic. The *Practical*, which contains the Tree of Life, is our concern here.
43 Acts 22 vii

the serpent into a stick that Moses performed.[44] Budge goes on to produce evidence that the Jews learned of the occult in Egypt, as there was nowhere else for them to have gained this knowledge.[45]

It is quite correct however, to state that the Qabalah is an Egyptian tradition contained within Hebrew wisdom. That the Qabalah contains elements of Jewish language and forms part of rabbinic doctrine seems self-evident. We should be grateful to the Jewish people for assuming guardianship of the Qabalistic wisdom and providing the Western Magical Tradition with such a powerful artefact. The renowned Eliphas Levi re-discovered the Qabalah centuries later and promoted its wisdom as a magical system. Levi certainly realized that within the Tree of Life lay a school of philosophy appropriate to the consciousness of the West.

W.G.Gray wrote extensively on the Qabalah. He suggested that its insight into the nature of the Divinity was invaluable, as it contains,

> …a very practical solution to the problem by affording no less than Ten *balanced* and perfectly harmonized God-persons. Each complements and equipoises with the others, so that they control each other's influence.[46]

The principles of the Qabalah are simple and complex at the same time. The student must realise that paradoxes are common in any esoteric study; they are there to help to instil the real essence of a particular wisdom. Two apparently conflicting elements give rise to a third, and that which is born contains the insight. This is the *triad*, a concept attributed to both Kant and Hegel. A thesis gives rise to an anti-thesis, and the two are melded into a synthesis. That may seem a prosaic concept, but it is a most valuable one when applied to the study of magic.

The Tree of Life

An understanding of the *Tree of Life* is essential for the student of magic, as it contains a microcosm of esoteric principles. The goal is, in the widest sense, to provide an analogy of the Divine.

---

44 E. Wallis Budge, *Egyptian Magic* (New York: Dover Publications, 1971) p.4,5
45 Budge p.23
46 W.G.Gray, *Working with Inner Light: The Magical Journal of William G. Gray* (Cheltenham: Skylight Press, 2010)

The Qabalah is understood to be linked to Hebraic cosmology. The ten Sephiroth correspond to the ten levels of creation, which should be understood as different perspectives of a single creator. In the Hebrew teachings, much is made of the 'revelations' of God in the sense of certain aspects of creation being hidden while others are 'revealed'. The notion of infinity is seen to be one that encompasses all aspects of creation, producing a total unity. This is not a polytheistic system; the Sephiroth are not separate gods, but successive points in a continual descent of divine energy toward manifestation on earth.

The Sephiroth are aligned in three pillars, a 'masculine' pillar of mercy, a 'feminine' pillar of severity and a middle pillar of equilibrium. Energy descends in the pattern of a lightning flash from the Godhead; it repeatedly criss-crosses from the right, masculine side of the tree to the left, feminine side and then descends toward the middle pillar where polarities are resolved. These are points of balance and unity without which manifestation cannot occur. The technique of achieving this end is the essence of Qabalistic magic.

The first task for the student is to realize the three separate states of existence – positive, negative and neutral. It is important that these three possibilities are thoroughly understood. Positive and negative are polarities, and neutral is the point of balance, thus neither is in the ascendant. Also, these are constantly changing, the one into the other.

Reflect upon the names of the left and right hand pillars – Mercy and Severity. Let it suffice that the Middle Pillar is seen as a place of repose and balance, while the other two pillars represent principles that are ever changing *in their degree*. We need to understand their nature if we are to incorporate these aspects of the world into ourselves. For our aim is to gain wholeness, through the Tree, and assimilate all.

It is also essential for the student not to regard the Tree as a static, two-dimensional diagram – energy is constantly flowing within it. If the Tree is visualized in three dimensions, its true essence becomes much more clear. Force flows up and down the Middle Pillar, but in a way that forms a loop, one that stretches out into a space beyond the Tree. A similar current moves clockwise from Sephira to Sephira to form an outer ring. These two paths of energy, two hoops moving within each other, construct a sphere. Other elements may be added, forming a third loop that moves horizontally across the others and providing even more of a solid form. Those who are inspired by this type of construction may wish to incorporate the paths between the spheres as well!

The Four Worlds

The system of the *Four Worlds* within the Qabalah has a twofold purpose. Firstly, to aid the student to recognise different aspects of each Sephira, and secondly, to provide an ordered approach to any study. Those who desire to employ any Sephira for magical workings would be wise to give much thought to the Four Worlds. This 'sub-division' enables the magician to isolate any particular energy that he requires within a particular Sephira.

The Names of Power, the basis of ceremonial magic, are contained herein. A more complex system involving the letters and associated numbers of the Hebrew alphabet also exists. Because of its complexity, this is beyond the scope of the present volume. However, those who would wish to pursue this line of study can only be encouraged to do so.

We are more concerned here with expanding our knowledge of the Sephiroth, and being familiar with the Four Worlds is of paramount importance. As already explained, we must do everything possible to charge all of the Ten Sephiroth with energy so that the Tree is not relegated to a flat, two-dimensional diagram.

To begin: *Assiah* is the physical sense; *Yetzirah*, the mental; *Briah*, the soul; *Atziluth*, the spirit. Certain Sephiroth are associated with each one of the worlds, but this is not an *equivalent* characteristic, it is an additional skein of meaning. Thus if we wish to employ the earthly characteristic (Assiah) of Netzach, which might be interpreted as sensual beauty, then we would concentrate upon that combination in our magical ritual.

The Ten Sephiroth

Malkuth

Malkuth is the Tenth Sephira – The Kingdom; its image is of a young woman crowned and throned. The picture is similar to the Tarot card,

The World. As the Sephira at the root of the Tree, it anchors the other nine; it does this by being true to its nature – that of earth and the material. All physical forms return to earth. Not one single atom is ever destroyed, it is transformed. The potential for change is as much present in Malkuth as in any other Sephira.

Yesod

Yesod is the Ninth Sephira – The Foundation. The image is of a beautiful, naked man. Independent and self-reliant, it corresponds to the virtues of the High Priestess of the Tarot. Although allied to the Moon, this Sephira has more than one nature, just as the Moon waxes and wanes. It both attracts, in its nurturing role, and retreats – into darkness and cold. The Moon is associated with romance, reflecting the joy lovers experience, although equally mirroring sadness and the sundering of intimacy. The Mother may also be cruel and reject her children. The Sephira of old magic, Yesod embodies at the same time the High Priestess and the sorceress.

Hod

Hod is the Eighth Sephira – Glory; the image is of a hermaphrodite. The virtues of the Magician of the Tarot are in this Sephira. The mind is at its zenith, capable of creating any vision and manifesting the same. There is a close association between Yesod, the preceding Sephira, and Hod. The relationship between Isis and Thoth is here. The god of magic and writing came, in turn, to the aid of Isis, Osiris and their son Horus. He was also the teacher of Isis, though many of the secrets of magic also came to her from Ra. Isis may have outwitted the great solar god, but she could never better Thoth. Much lunar imagery is within Thoth. In his later transformation into Hermes, this was lost.

Netzach

Netzach is the Seventh Sephira – Victory. The image is of a beautiful naked woman. The object of desire – Venus or Aphrodite. This Sephira is associated with sensual pleasure, and also the arts. Beauty is truth, from where springs the noble thought, the magnificent work. The artist knows he must woo his muse, and in return she will give him inspiration. Netzach knows that indulgence is not joy, and she works hard to retain a sense of balance.

Tiphareth

Tiphareth is the Sixth Sephira – Beauty. Its image is that of a majestic king or a child. The Tarot card of The Sun has a strong link with this Sephira. King Oak and John Barleycorn are two mythical English figures associated with Tiphareth, along with archetypes such as Mithras and Osiris, for sacrifice is at the heart of this Sephira. The lotus flower opens and the self disappears, the innocence of the child returns.

Geburah

Geburah is the Fifth Sephira – Severity. Its image is of a warrior in his chariot. Geburah is known as the 'warrior of God' because of his divine purpose. He carries justice and power in his sword. His affinity with Horus, and also Anubis, is also marked. Geburah strikes where it is necessary, not cruelly, but with precision and might.

Chesed

Chesed is the Fourth Sephira – Mercy. The image is of a king upon his throne. The monarch's generosity to those of his kingdom is legendary, and all love him for that quality. His is the exuberance of youth and the compassion of age. His laughter and joviality fill the air, and all prosper who inhabit his realm. Optimism is unbounded in this Sephira – never degenerating into foolishness. Chesed is the sphere of the true visionary, one inspired only by the divine, walking constantly with angels.

Binah

Binah is the Third Sephira – Understanding. Its image is of a mature woman. The keyword of this Sephira is 'patience'. Timeless, with limitless understanding, all extremes of emotion are present in some form or another. Binah is no stranger to sorrow or to ecstasy. Nothing of the world, present or past, surprises her – she is Time itself. Yesod shares her maternal essence, but that quality in Binah is totally universal. Deep and profound, she is known as 'the great sea'. All creation came from her vast and endless waters, and Binah will continue to give birth to all feelings, all existence, unto eternity.

Chokmah

Chokmah is the Second Sephira – Wisdom. The image is a bearded man. This Sephira represents all the parts of the universe that make up the whole. Chokmah is the entirety of creation, the physical aspect of the whole tree. His wisdom springs from experience; he knows all aspects of man and woman. He is Sophia, the spirit of Wisdom. This paradox should make us realise that Chokmah has a universal power, not just one that has male or female origins. This force springs from Kether and is manifest as the visible world. Its nature is divine – ineffable, invincible.

Kether

Kether is the First Sephira – The Crown. Its image is an ancient bearded king in profile. The king is in profile because his features cannot be seen by man. For his eyes to rest upon the divine is too much for mortal man; he shrivels and dies in its presence. As Yahweh informs Moses, 'Thou canst not see my face: for there shall no man see me, and live.' [47] Man must seek a oneness with God, something he may achieve with contemplation and meditation. By experiencing the divine by degrees, he will gradually absorb its nature. The magician knows that he must become the god he seeks to invoke, nothing less will do. Kether is the point of creation. Other states exist beyond it, perhaps just as significant, as we shall discover.

The Three Veils, Daath and The Qliphoth

Three worlds lie in an arc beyond Kether – the 'Veils of Negative Existence'. This definition of limitless space embraces the idea of the actual moment when the unmanifested becomes the manifested. One

---

47 Exodus 33, v.20

of the principal themes of the Qabalah is the interaction between the spiritual and material worlds. We need our senses in order to experience the material world, but it does not follow that they enable us to perceive it accurately. The Eastern School unequivocally states that the seeker always risks being deceived by the senses.

Daath is the shadowy sphere that lies between Tiphareth and Kether. It has been defined as 'the pit of chaos', the receptacle for the mistakes of God. After being expelled from the psyche, all spiritual rubbish resides here. It is the 'limbo' of the Christian Church. On a cosmological level, it is from the waste matter of Daath that other universes are created in the unknown.

In the Arthurian legends, Lancelot must cross the 'Bridge of Swords' in order to reach his salvation in Guinevere. The Bridge represents the harmful aspects of ourselves, our ignoble thoughts, lying in wait below. We must walk upon the sword of Geburah, and are given the rod of Chesed to aid us in keeping our balance. The *Upanishads* warn of this path:

> A sharpened edge of a razor, hard to traverse,
> A difficult path it is this – poets declare! [48]

Daath also represents the Dweller upon the Threshold, the Watcher at the Gate, the figure that will not let the seeker pass until he has proved his worthiness to do so. Our motives betray us, and if we are not certain of the reasons why we wish to journey to the Kingdom, then we will be refused entry. Gray's view is that the consciousness has no experience and must learn 'the hard way'.

The *Qliphoth*, like Daath, also lies in the depths of darkness. Every force, magical or otherwise, has its adverse aspect. Virtues may become vices more easily than we could suspect. The Qliphoth, being an unbalanced and destructive representation of the Tree, represent a positive evil. It is important to differentiate between 'positive' and 'negative' evil. The former stand against evolution and progress, the latter merely opposes an idea. For balance to be maintained in society there must be the opportunity for the questioning of principles. Such a notion may be described as a 'negative evil' and is beneficial, if not essential.

---

48   Robert Ernest Hume, *The Thirteen Principal Upanishads, translated from Sanskrit* (Oxford: OUP, 1931)

In mainstream politics, for example, it is a radical or a reactionary view alternately asserting itself. The foundation of an ordered society is a genuine democracy of thought; the opposite is tyranny and oppression.

The Paths upon the Tree of Life

Between the Sephiroth lie the Paths, each of which has a title and a Tarot card of the Major Arcana assigned to it. Much of what was originally written about the paths was made deliberately opaque. This is because *pathworking* is a magical exercise and occultists of the time were anxious to conceal certain methods from those who were not initiates. The journey from one Sephira to another can be a very powerful experience. Alan Richardson[49] has described a method of meditation which is most effective.

The student should realize that balancing a sphere, both within itself and with another, is far more than just an intellectual exercise. *It is the practical application of the principles revealed.* If, after studying the Qabalah, we do not act in a compassionate and thoughtful way then its lessons are worthless. As Richard Cavendish explains,

> ...experiences tend to be grist to the magician's mill...the magician must experience and reconcile every aspect of 'the All' in himself... [50]

---

49 Details of the method are given in: Alan Richardson, *The Magician's Tables – A Complete Book of Correspondences* (London: Godsfield Press, 2007) p.83
50 Richard Cavendish, *Man Myth and Magic* (1970, Vol. 3)

The Western Magical Tradition

It seems as if much of our sub-conscious mind carries on from incarnation to incarnation, it is the conscious mind only that we build again with each life.

Dion Fortune

The roots of the Western Magical tradition are in Ancient Egypt, Chaldea, and Classical Greece. Much ancient wisdom must have been exclusively within an oral tradition, so it may be that much has been lost. Perhaps what remains is merely a pale shadow of what was magic in those times. Schools of philosophy and religion abounded in the ancient world, as temples both public and private were an accepted feature of the times. A hierarchy of beliefs was evident, most evident in the concealing of the Mysteries from the common gaze. Sacred dramas were performed, the most celebrated being those of Isis, and a system of initiation existed, one which was highly secret.

It was the Arab world that preserved these traditions after the fall of Rome. The Jews brought the Qabalah to Western Europe; many Medieval grimoires have a Qabalistic influence. Contact between Christian and Muslim at the time of the Crusades ensured a homogenous wisdom developed. The Cathars preserved much knowledge until their persecution by the Church in Europe brought about their demise. The Rosicrucians and Freemasons were the later guardians of these mysteries.

The Golden Dawn is credited with establishing the 'western magical tradition'. The title is used to delineate a particular school of occult practice, one entirely removed from any Eastern tradition. To have lived in England in the 1880s meant it was possible to be a member of an organisation that offered initiation into the esoteric world. The celebrated Golden Dawn set out to be a Victorian 'occult academy' and this ambition made it a revolutionary organisation. It was also offering instruction to both men and women, and this was the main aspect that made it different from any magical organisation that had gone before.

Its genesis was prompted by several factors, one of which was likely to have been an unconscious reaction to the doctrine of the Theosophical Society. Blavatsky in her writings makes it plain that she does not look kindly upon any other spiritual tradition than Buddhism. The emphasis upon the Oriental willingness to accept fate as the arbiter of all temporal existence has never been wholeheartedly accepted in the West.

The Western Magical Tradition has at its heart a desire to enquire about the nature of existence. Occultists in the West have always experimented with the forces that they consider are controlling the universe. Their efforts must naturally comply with the Divine Will in order to succeed. Even if they fail however, the will to achieve becomes stronger, as does steel when it is tempered in the flames.

The realisation that a school of magic could be gleaned from what already existed nearer home brought a new exuberance to Western occultism. Its basis would be found in the philosophy of Ancient Greece, the knowledge of Sumeria and Chaldea and the wisdom of Ancient Egypt. The fabled Atlantis also had a part to play.

The supernatural aspect of Britain was preserved in the druidic lore, and the wizardry of Merlin. In Northern Europe, the Norse myths typify the milieu of gods, kings and heroes intrinsic to the harsh reality of the setting. The kingdom of Avalon has within it the powerful Arthurian symbolism of the Knights' Quest for the Grail. We can now see how the Western way is active – combining the nobility of the warrior with the ambiance of fairies and spirits. This approach is in contrast to the passive ways of the East, where the warm climate almost shapes the mystical approach.

With the increasing interest in mysticism that occurred in the late 1960s it was the ways of the East that were most attractive to Western youth. Did not the Fabulous Orient disregard the material and the intellectual and consider only the transcendental? This path seemed in every way superior to anything the West could offer in the spiritual stakes. An absence of *thinking* (particularly about the means to earn a living) for a time appealed to the dreamy Celt and the anarchic Anglo-Saxon. Combining this philosophy with potent hashish from Afghanistan and psychedelic drugs resulted in a world dominated by gurus and flying saucers.

In the next two decades, the New Age became prominent in the 'mystical' culture. Though extremely eclectic in its approach, this new 'movement' embraced the pagan, the druidic and the Arthurian in equal measure. Technology was to play its part, as the digital revolution spread from America throughout the West. Science too had its part to play, as researchers in the fields of cosmology and neurology were discovering that consciousness was the source of all that we perceive, so that metaphysics and quantum physics suddenly became allies.

The Kingdom of Avalon

'Myth' has a great significance in the workings of the human consciousness and unconscious. The Arthuriad is a great if not *the greatest* tale that we may ever know in our inner being. It is rich in meaning and,

> It is because of this unique run through from the depths to the heights, from beginnings to endings, from elemental to spiritual that the Arthurian legends are of unique importance. No other system has this complete range in such detail and ramification.[51]

This contribution to the Western Tradition cannot be ignored; neither can its significance to the individual's unconscious, particularly those who would involve themselves in the great tradition of magic. As Jung makes clear,

> It is not the part which can be externally and biographically dated that constitutes the real life of a person, but its myth – the fateful, spiritual inner side of life.[52]

The saga is eminently suited to magical workings because the interplay of its symbolism is original and therefore has its own potency. The

51 Knight, *ibid.*, p.240
52 Jung, *ibid.*, p.166

figures, situations and truths are not allegorical, meaning that they have no comparison with existing individuals. As Alan Richardson tell us,

> ...the tales within the Arthurian Cycle contain fragments of occult lore of incredible age, and [that] Arthur, Morgan le Fay and the rest were hereditary initiatic titles rather than specific historical personages.[53]

King Arthur and Merlin are mentioned in the medieval text, *The Black Book of Carmarthen*, and the very landscape of Britain itself was described thus in *Vita Merlini – The Life of Merlin*. The section entitled *The Creation of the Work* particularly mentions 'islands'.

Britain is said to be the foremost and best of these, producing in its fruitfulness every single thing. For it bears crops which throughout the year give the noble gifts of fragrance for the use of man, and it has woods and glades with honey dripping in them, and lofty mountains and broad green fields, fountains and rivers, fishes and cattle and wild beasts, fruit trees, gems, precious metals, and whatever else creative nature is in the habit of furnishing.

Merlin

Merlin, as the first and greatest magician, employed the power of the earth for his wizardry. He came from an age when the old gods were chaos, old night and the Unmanifest – the sources of ancient magic. Thus Merlin was familiar with earth energies, the material form of the ethereal, and used them, very successfully indeed. He is magic personified, depicted as The Magician of the Tarot. He who stands with arm upraised bringing down power from Heaven and directing it earthward.

Merlin is the Shape Shifter and the Trickster – quicksilver – Mercury. He shows us how to use a situation to our advantage, how to control it – rather than be at the mercy of fickle fate. No force or foe has mastery over Merlin. He is the spirit of the dragon and the snake, the symbols of wisdom. It is the *wisdom of the Fool*.

Shakespeare included the character of a fool in many of his plays. As a dramatic device, the presence of the fool is invaluable because

---

53   Alan Richardson, *ibid.*, p.107

he may 'speak out of turn' as often as he wishes. His view is always pertinent too, because it has no hidden agenda. The fool sees the truth, perhaps because he is no fool at all. The only real madness is to consider that the world is subject to the rules of logic. Reason can only take us so far, and never far enough.

Christ is the 'Holy Fool', because he innocently lives out the way of the Divine. The Fool represents a state of ease, one that precedes enlightenment. It only takes a slight movement, a twitch upon the veil, for The Fool to slip into the otherworld. He occupies that elusive 'present' that becomes 'past' as soon as we choose to contemplate the moment. The Fool, like The Magician, lives eternally in the present, and has no truck with either the past or the future.

The Fool has no identity, or conversely he may display every possible trait that a personality might own, will own, or ever wish to own. The Fool is all and one together. The Fool is eccentric; he is 'the nutty professor', the genius, the artist and the visionary. His elevated state of awareness enables him to grasp the unity within chaos. He accepts that the apparently haphazard events which make up existence are merely illusions, and that behind the veil lies 'something entirely different'.

King Arthur

In King Arthur we encounter not only the warrior *in excelsis* but the Sun God and the Sacrificial God. The correspondence between the Egyptian myth of Ra's nightly journey to rise once more as the sun, and the aspect of resurrection in the Arthurian Myth is most obvious. Arthur is a figure of light bestowing warmth and healing onto every part of his kingdom. In the divine plan every one of us is his subject, yet *he serves us*.

Paying homage to any figure of authority has gone out of fashion, yet the magician must know what it is like to rule and to obey. We all have a master, even the chosen ones. The magician is also a god, for he walks with gods and feels himself to be an equal in their company. The mortal and immortal have become one.

We call on the powers to serve us, and only if the heart is pure will they serve us. No other way will do, for there should be no half-measures regarding the power of gods and kings. If we are of the light, nothing will be denied us. We should see the world with the clear eye of the child. All that is blessed with the light of the sun is touched with heavenly gold. The sun is life, beauty and truth. Sol permits no shadow and he is as beautiful at dawn as he is in the evening. We should remember that with magic we get what we need not always what we want.

No matter how much earthly dominion he may have, the king knows his end awaits him in his physical death. Arthur realises that his going from this plane merely signifies the beginning of a journey to the otherworld. Earthly power, by its very nature, must only be temporal, and it is the way of things that they must perish. Yet beyond Death is a state of unconditional love, and knowing this gives us a great strength. Like the phoenix rising from the ashes, life returns as part of an eternal cycle.

The relationship between Arthur and Merlin is symbiotic, each needs the other. Jung's definition of 'the hero' seems to contain elements of both figures.

> The hero represents man's unconscious self. This appears empirically as the sum total and the quintessence of all archetypes, and thus it also includes the type of the 'father', that is, the wise old man. In this sense the hero is his own father, and begets himself.[54]

The Three Queens

Dion Fortune[55] spent most of her life in devotion to the Goddess. She particularly related the more obvious qualities of the feminine to *The Three Queens* of the Arthuriad. In some traditions Morgan le Fay and Nimuë, The Lady of the Lake, are regarded as one, while Guinevere is depicted as *Mother Nature* – the May Queen – all sumptuous blossom and growth. Dion Fortune attempts to define the changing mood of The Goddess:

> The daughter of the Great Mother is Persephone, Queen of Hades, ruler of the kingdoms of sleep and death. Under the form of the Dark Queen men also worship her who is the One: likewise is she Aphrodite. And

---

54 Jung, *ibid.*, p.36
55 Dion Fortune had a great affection for Avalon and founded a magical commune at Chalice Orchard in Glastonbury. She is also buried there, in the area known as Bovetown.

herein is a great mystery, for it is decreed that none shall understand the one without the other.[56]

The Goddess has the power to cause the tides to rise and fall, but she is also the cruel sea. Within her are cold and ruthless emotions; she is Circe who, without a qualm, leads the sailors to their doom. Morgan le Fay (perhaps in another incarnation – Morrigan) is the personification of the Dark Goddess. She is in legend Arthur's half sister with whom he had an incestuous relationship, one that bore Mordred. 'Fay' (Fairy) refers to an other-worldly figure,

> ...tall, commanding and seductively beautiful. Dominating, ruthless, sensual and unpredictable... sometimes benevolent... sometimes cruel... (with) formidable magical powers...[57]

When Arthur takes Guinevere as his queen, Morgan le Fay seeks eternal revenge. She even attempts to steal Excalibur, the symbol of his power. She fails to take the sword but makes off with the sheath, an act just as damaging, as from this moment on the fortunes of Arthur begin to decline. Logres will be rent with dissension and the Grail will not be won, causing the kingdom to become the Waste Land.

Morgan le Fay is the 'enchantress' of the Romances. Richard Cavendish explains this *leitmotif*:

> ...a hero in danger from an enchantress, who desires him, hates him, or both...is related to the old and widespread theme of the evilness of woman, which is linked with her sexual allure. The enchantress wants either to kill the hero...or more often to do away with him metaphorically by keeping him prisoner in her own realm, so preventing him from pursuing his own career in the world. She entangles him in a web of mindless sensual pleasure, in which he loses his capacity for action. The encounter with the *femme fatale* is one of the perils which the true hero must experience and survive.[58]

Morgan le Fay was, ironically perhaps, once the pupil of Merlin. She is described by Malory as 'a clerk of necromancy'. Another medieval

---

56   Fortune, *ibid.*, p.130

57   Richard Cavendish, *King Arthur & The Grail – The Arthurian Legends and their Meaning* (London: Weidenfeld and Nicholson, 1978) p.44

58   Cavendish, *ibid.*, p.52

chronicler, Geoffrey of Monmouth does not ascribe sorcery to Morgan, merely noting that, 'She...knows an art by which to change her shape, and to cleave the air on new wings like Daedalus.'

She brings Arthur to Avalon (seen as the realm of King Avallach, perhaps Morgan's father) when he is dying. With her nine maidens (or *Morgens*) Morgan nurses the king.[59] Because of her association with the end of Arthur, she is seen as the bringer of Death.

If the apprentice magician invokes the energy of Morgan le Fay inevitably he will travel to faraway places, strange and unfamiliar. He should take care not to stray into realms that may simply be *fascinating*, for the Goddess forever tests us, in particular the rightness of our perceptions. Her love is unconditional and the Goddess expects us to act in the same way with her. We must accept *all* her ways – from the terrible to the sublime. She is the mirrored lake as well as the fathomless ocean. Her love is endless and eternal – as are all her passions. Within her heart are all memories and all deeds. It is the role of the Goddess to accept all and, because of this, she forgives us again and again. We are all her children.

The Grail

Elements of Atlantis are reflected in the kingdom of Avalon, wherein lies the Grail. The Knights of the Round Table embark upon their eternal Quest, trusting that they will achieve their goal. In the same way the magus believes that the truth is to be found in the kingdom that lies beyond the veil. It will be a valuable exercise to compare the nature of the Questing Knight and the Magus.

An enormous amount of material exists with regard to the Grail, which is only to be expected, for it is the most prominent symbol in the Western Mysteries. In brief, we may say that it is the zenith of love and perfection, an idea rather than an object, and reflects our own personal search for significance in our existence. The knight is asked this question:

---

59 The Grail may have been guarded by a different number of maidens. It is possible that they totalled nine. 'The breath of nine maidens keeps it boiling' is a reference to Annwn's Cauldron in a poem by Taliesin (Grigsby, p.194) Graves suggests these may be a manifestation of the nine daughters of Zeus.

'Why do you seek?'
He replies:
'I desire to know in order to serve.'

These are the same sentiments that are voiced when the initiate is quizzed as to his motives for desiring the mysteries to be revealed to him.

The student would do well to reflect upon this interchange deeply, for it is the only true reason for the learning and practice of magic.

Whatever the Grail might be – artefact, vision, or idea – it relies for its actual existence on being perceived by man. It may well have been present in some form in the universe millions upon millions of years before the advent of *homo sapiens*. Consider the Grail, as well as being eternal, as something that also reflects the essence of those who lived in a particular era. Times change and we change with them, so our notion of the Grail alters constantly.

The Grail is a microcosm of the universe, and so completely at one with it that its form is indistinguishable from those things we experience in our own consciousness. More than an actual object existing in a specific time and place, the Grail is a metaphysical event. The Grail too is a symbol implanted deep in the collective *unconscious*. Because the Grail remains hidden from view it is somehow regarded by the dull as suspect, or subversive.

The subtle element in things, as the occult so patently is, runs counter to much modern thinking. The obvious and the crass are everywhere reflected in the 'entertainment' we are offered. Our society also has an endless hunger for access to every gobbet of information. We are not permitted to have secrets – the State and the media does not approve. Thus, the Grail as a symbol is transformed once again – it becomes a symbol of eccentricity, even rebellion.

Consider how we might perceive the Grail, or King Arthur, if we had the good fortune to encounter either of them. Powerful entities project their own – equally powerful – aura, irrespective of their location in space and time. The images they create exist for all time. Thus, we may 'see' a great many extraordinary things that are associated with these archetypes, or even an all-absorbing vision of the original.

As Camelot is the perfect place, so the Grail is the most perfect idea. The Grail is a symbol of all that we desire to cherish and preserve during our sojourn on this planet – our home. The universe responds to strength, never to weakness, and the resolve that is shown by those engaged upon the Quest is rewarded with 'the peace that passeth understanding'. The Grail heals our pain no matter how grievous it may be when it was inflicted upon us.

Beyond the state of ecstasy that the Grail brings lies the ineffable. It is a sight that we should perhaps not experience in all its totality, for it may be too much for us. The Grail exists in an infinite number of forms, and perhaps we are shown the version that is best suited to ourselves – a 'likeness' of the Holy Vessel that best reflects our progress along the path.

Some magical workings have succeeded in evoking Arthurian archetypes so successfully that they could be seen walking among the company. They almost have a desire to be seen. As Gareth Knight tells us:

> Those who work on the inner planes need help from us even as we need help from them, for the whole creation is joined together. No part is meant to work alone.[60]

Yet, no magician, no matter how experienced, should underestimate their power.

Sacred Sites

It seems more than likely that Neolithic man sensed the inherent power in certain places upon the Earth and marked that discovery by constructing his monuments there. It is a case of the land choosing the people rather than the other way round. The ancients would too have instinctively been 'in touch' with the sentient spirits that reside in these 'places of power'. In many cases these forces are still present today at sites. If the visitor feels the presence of a guardian, acknowledging their presence and showing respect is not only advisable but necessary.

Megalithic stones stand as sentinels of space and time, gathering and sustaining the power of the earth. It is more *logical* to believe that there are spirits of the earth in these locations than to deny their existence. When we are inspired or even overwhelmed by the beauty

---

60 Knight, *ibid.*, p.282

of some place, then its essence has in some way been transmitted to us. We may be aware of other even more profound qualities personified in an actual spirit in that location. Whether we are aware of its material presence or we experience visions of it makes little difference, it still 'exists'.

The 'psychic' nature of the individual may determine how intense that feeling is, and it is obvious that some people are more 'tuned in' to 'sacred places' than others. What is particularly significant in Britain is that these megalithic monuments – stone circles, standing stones, long barrows, hills and 'forts' – resonate deep in the native psyche. It is as if the landscape is a physical map that echoes our soul.

The existence of 'ley lines' (a plotted route between two historical sites) is a very different concept to 'energy lines'. The latter refers to paths of force that can be discerned by employing the method of dowsing. Particularly sensitive areas often occur at the crossing of underground streams – called 'juvenile water' – and lightning will often strike at these points because it is the most conducive place to ground its energy.

The view that stone circles reflect the heavens seems somehow obvious. To our ancestors the nightly appearance of the moon and stars must have seemed purposeful and significant. The phases of the moon and the lessening of the hours of daylight as the year neared the Winter solstice must also have been noted. Whether stone circles and long barrows were specifically constructed to align with features in the heavens at a given time in the year is a subject discussed endlessly by those who study *archaeoastronomy*. The general consensus among these worthy gentlemen seems to be that at some sites this is assuredly the case, whereas at others it is more doubtful.

To my mind the greatest fascination is speculating upon the mindset of the people who set about planning and constructing these great edifices. They had very limited language, but they must have had leaders – those who could inspire others by gesture and example to achieve their personal vision. Similar perhaps to the great movie directors of our own times, they too were magicians in their way.

It is apposite here to mention the methods of Tibetan monks who were witnessed, as late as the 1930s, engaged upon levitating blocks of stone using only sound. This astonishing feat was apparently achieved by groups of monks playing trumpets and drums who could, by this means, move a block weighing four tons into the air. It was said that by the same means physical matter could also be made to dissolve or disintegrate.

While researching *Spirits of the Stones* (a compendium of recollections and impressions of Neolithic places) the author, Alan Richardson, had this personal revelation.

> As I got deeper and deeper into the images and energies behind the hitherto private experiences of many quite remarkable individuals, I found myself becoming strangely moved. It was as if part of me, long since lost at the back of my mind, were being made to remember things that I should never have forgotten.[61]

Feelings of *déjà-vu* when sacred sites are visited indicates the strong sense of 'past lives' that every individual holds whether they are conscious of this or not. We could also mention 'future lives', as ones 'being' shifts both backwards and forwards along a time line that is probably not linear in any case. Having a formal 'regression' or simply experiencing intensely the presence of a previous incarnation may give us valuable personal insights. The ancients revered the ancestors and all those who had gone before, and rightly so too. They worshipped them in a way that was dignified and had a more robust and glorious view of death than we have. A continuing journey was how they viewed the end of the earthly existence rather than finality, or any reason for grief. Jung suggests that:

> The psyche is not of today! Its age is measured in many millions of years. Individual consciousness is only the flower and fruit of a season...[62]

Plants, crystals, and the stones from which megalithic monuments are constructed have much power, because they are the material expression of the spiritual. It would be an error to believe that the material world is devoid of any transcendental qualities, as certain Christian cults have done. Mother Nature, or Gaia, represents the realm of dense matter as *Malkuth* is the anchoring sphere upon the *Tree of Life*, and is referred to as 'The Kingdom' or 'The Meadows of Asphodel'. Malkuth is simply

---

61 Alan Richardson, *Spirits of the Stones: Visions of Sacred Britain* (London: Virgin, 2001) p.104
62 Jung, *ibid.*, p.12

one point on the journey towards *Kether – The Crown*. The path may lead from the densest matter to absolute spirit or it may be followed in an opposite direction. P.D. Ouspensky likens Malkuth to the Sphinx, who:

> …with its riddle…devoured those who approached it and could not solve the riddle. The allegory of the Sphinx means that there are questions of a certain order which man must not approach unless he knows how to answer them. Having once come into contact with certain ideas man is unable to live as he lived before; he must either go further or perish under a burden which is too heavy for him.[63]

Christian places of worship were later constructed at pagan sites, mostly with the intention of eradicating the original energy, but on some occasions attempting to harness it. Chartres Cathedral in Central France has an extraordinary ambiance, one that combines several different kinds of spiritual energy. Added to this, the high altar is built upon the confluence of twenty-seven underground waterways!

Faith and prayer are powerful forces. To imply that billions of worshippers of a dozen different creeds were, over the centuries, committing a fundamental error is unreasonable. Even if belief only moves metaphorical mountains, that is still impressive. Places of worship have a profound effect upon those who visit them, and not solely because of their architectural magnificence. An invisible presence is evident at any site where devotion has been offered. One might consider together Chartres Cathedral and Mount Shasta in Northern California; both places have an extraordinary power. The one is allied to the Catholic faith, the other to Native American shamanism; both were equally sacred to their followers.

---

63   P.D. Ouspensky, *In Search of the Miraculous* (Orlando: Harcourt, 1949) p.214

5

Ancient Egyptian Magic

I am everything that has been, and is, and will be, and my veil no mortal has uncovered.

Inscription upon the Temple of Isis at Sais

The Egyptian pantheon of gods is eminently suited to magical working. The powers of Isis, Thoth, and Horus have been employed by magicians for centuries, thus their presence is exceptionally potent upon the Inner Planes. It should be emphasized that these deities represent forces of extreme power and must not to be taken lightly. The gods and goddesses of Ancient Egypt should be awarded the greatest respect and offered the utmost devotion. No less will do. Their presence in the temple or place of working will be immense, and felt most strongly by the magician.

Egyptian magic is *natural magic* in the sense of *theurgy* – the invoking of power from gods rather than spirits. These are ancient energies, and one glance at how they were depicted in statues and wall paintings should suffice to indicate their immense influence upon those who created them. The principle of *ka*, of an energy that is separate yet sustaining of the individual, is an intrinsic element of Egyptian magic.[64] Jung had this to say of it:

> ...an expression of the creative and preserving power of life; in earliest times it referred specifically to the masculine powers of procreation...it was applied to spiritual and psychic power... The *ka* was born together with the person. [65]

---

64 For more information, see Alan Richardson, *Magical Gateways* (Minnesota: Llewellyn Publications, 1992)
65 Jung, *ibid.*, p.185

The 'Ka posture' is an essential gesture in any 'Egyptian' ritual, as it channels power from above and into the heart of the magician. Combined with simple breathing exercises and being aware of the magical centres of the body – the genitals, the solar plexus, and the throat – the Ka posture will bring a column of light down from above and into the temple or the place of working.

A thorough knowledge of the nature of the principal deities – Ra, Horus, Isis and Thoth – is absolutely essential before the student even considers using their presence in any temple working. Other deities – Anubis, Osiris, Hathor, Maat and Sekhmet – should also be thoroughly investigated, so that the individual characteristics and the manner in which all these deities interact is clearly understood.

The magician follows the ways of gods, not men. The conduct of the magician is always faultless. Only by standing fully in the light will it be possible for heaven to beam its full power upon him. *Thoth* has the title of 'the mind of God'. His consort *Maat* is the Goddess of Truth. Together this should indicate clearly, and without the slightest doubt, what is at the heart of magic. Thus, the student must be constantly aware of his every word, thought and deed. Whatever passes through the mind always leaves its mark, so discrimination and diligence is essential for the magician.

Ra and Nuit

Ra is the creator god and naturally identified with the Sun, later with Horus, another sky deity who, as a falcon, had within his power the sun and the moon. Horus sits upon the shoulder of Ra and is the instrument of his will and his protector.

Nuit, or Nut, is the goddess of the sky who brings about the rebirth of the sun every morning. She is covered in stars and holds the title of *She who holds a thousand souls*. Nuit symbolises resurrection, and swallows the sun every night. This traverses her belly through the night and emerges from her uterus in the morning. Osiris, the sacrificial god, enters her heavens by means of a ladder, an ancient symbol of protection. By rising into the highest domains, Osiris will eventually be resurrected. The role of Nuit, as well as a friend to all, was as a barrier separating the forces of chaos from the ordered world below her.

She was paired with Geb, the Earth, and her children were Osiris, Isis, Set, Nephthys and Horus: some of the most powerful of the Egyptian deities. It is said that originally Nuit and Geb were in a state of permanent sexual union. Ra ordered them to cease, temporarily, so that the world might be created!

Thoth and Anubis

The god of Magic and Writing is eminently suitable for any occult working. Thoth, as the advisor, arbitrator and helper of the gods, occupies a position of great power. It is Thoth who maintains the balance of power between good and evil, an essential task because he perceives, rightly, that neither one should ever dominate in the universe.

Among his great deeds, Thoth aided Isis to restore the dismembered Osiris, and brought Horus back to life after he had been slain. As the 'Voice of Ra', Thoth brought the universe into being. Thoth can be seen as the *Logos* of Plato, the heart of God, not just the means by which the will of Ra is translated into speech.

Thoth and his partner Maat stand each side of *Mandjet* the solar boat (The Boat of Millions of Years) when it crosses the sky in the morning and the underworld at night. Ra is accompanied by various other deities, the most efficacious being Set who regularly overcomes the serpent Apophis who attempts to halt the progress of the boat.

Originally a lunar god, Thoth personifies, through the phases of the moon, the procession of time. The curved beak of his ibis head can be seen to resemble the crescent moon. Thoth is also associated with the baboon, a nocturnal animal of great intelligence who 'sang' to the Moon.

Thoth is credited with inventing measurement and the calendar.[66] Thus he can be seen as bringing order unto chaos. The knowledge of Thoth is said to be written in a book,[67] hidden from all. It was said that by reading this work:

> …you will learn the language of beasts, how to see the wind and how to hear the sun, the secrets of the gods and the songs of the stars.[68]

---

66 The year is divided into thirty-six ten day periods, which was also the basis of Egyptian astrology. Thoth later adjusts this total, to add the missing five days.
67 Crowley believed this to be the Tarot and referred to the cards as 'The Book of Thoth'.
68 Versluis, *ibid.*, p.78

The later association of Thoth and Hermes may have been convenient to alter culture, but a certain amount of the original spirit of Thoth is lost in the exercise. Hermes is a messenger to the gods not a god himself. We shall learn of the nature of Hermetic magic later in our study.

Anubis travels to and from the underworld, and with Thoth and Osiris, he judges the dead. His title is 'Opener of the Way', and 'Lord of the Underworld', and he is also 'Guardian of the Scales'. Anubis dictates the fate of souls when they are weighed against the feather of 'truth' of Maat. He is the son of Osiris and Nephthys.

Isis

Thoth is the teacher of Isis, and thus magic is her domain. Isis is the very essence of the Goddess personified – the female mysteries, and the keeper of the veil. As Dion Fortune reminds us, 'All these goddesses are one goddess, and we call her Isis…'[69] Men who are adverse to the notion of a female owning power will never share in the secrets of the Goddess. To this end, those who do not have a true affinity with *the anima* cannot hope to fully enter into the nature of existence. As Jung propounded:

> The anima is in contact with the objects of the inner reality – the images of the collective unconscious – as the persona is in contact with the objects of external reality. The anima is an archetypal figure that might almost be described as the precipitate of man's age-long impressions of woman – not his conscious reasoned ideas, but the unconscious inherited mould into which she is cast.[70]

The predecessor of Isis was *Hathor* – 'lady of the sycamore' – and in her nature resides one aspect of the female psyche – for she is *lust*. It must be acknowledged that the Goddess has many faces. To the Celts she was the tripartite goddess, the eternal virgin, the bride, and the crone.

Inevitably, and indubitably, the feminine nature cannot be subdued. The untameable desire of the Goddess to unite with the God, and her triumph when she accomplishes this union, releases a wild, even terrifying force. It is only the fearless warrior that she wishes to couple

69   Fortune, *ibid.,* p.131
70   Corrie, Joan, *ABC of Jung's Psychology* (London: Kegan Paul, 1985) p.75

with, none other. Courage and strength are the only virtues that she admires and she knows them intimately for she possesses those qualities herself. As the sorcerer Don Juan reminds us,

> …women have a most fierce intensity. They can, therefore, reproduce an animal form with flair, ease, and a matchless ferocity.[71]

Thoth knows the nature of Isis his pupil and senses her absolute purity: '…she is the matrix of matter, the root substance of all existence, undifferentiated, pure.'[72] Thus he is aware of her role in the birth of the universe. In their union the Magician and the High Priestess become so at one with the universe that they become every atom within it. Both understand the cosmos *in its real aspect.*

The loop of the Ankh, the symbol of life, protection and eternity, is held by the gods of Ancient Egypt. It is associated with Isis and Osiris, the male and female – the womb and lingam joined to form life. Thoth, being the god of magic, holds a staff of authority as well as the ankh. The magician's staff is a symbol of power and a means of practising magic. We are reminded of Merlin's staff and perhaps that of Gandalf also.

Egyptian Themes

Cats, scorpions and the scarab beetle seem unlikely bedfellows, but they were all creatures highly revered in Ancient Egypt. The cat was domesticated in that country in 2000 BC,[73] and the goddesses with a physical appearance of the cat were Miu, Mafdet and Bestet. The most forbidding was Sekhmet the daughter of Ra. Her title was 'One before whom evil trembles', and it was believed her breath created the desert.

The scorpion goddess was Serket who was seen as one who stings the unrighteous yet cures those afflicted with bites from snakes and scorpions. The *Nefert* ('transformation', 'what has come into being') was the scarab beetle, who was thought to roll the sun above the horizon.

---

71 Castaneda, *ibid.*, p.137
72 Fortune, *ibid.*, p.130
73 Woe betide any who harmed a feline! Dire penalties were meted out to the offender.

6

The Way of the Shaman

A warrior considers himself already dead, so there is nothing to lose.

Carlos Castaneda

One way of magic which stands apart from the Western tradition is that of Shamanism. Unfortunately, the term 'shaman' has now been degraded, in the same way that the word 'spiritual' is now a catch-all description of New Age hobbies and pastimes. A genuine shaman, one who has inherited and absorbed the practice of sorcery, is a rare item. Those who in the modern day write with apparent knowledge of the practice are more often than not referring to some personal fantasy of their own.

'Shaman' was once a title known only to a few anthropologists and referred to any belief or practice that involved communication with the spirit world. Indeed, the fundamental ethos of shamanism is that the practitioner is an intermediary or messenger from the human world. The purpose of the shaman visiting these supernatural realms is to discover what is ailing the soul of a community or an individual. The shaman heals the physical body of those who are ailing by 'mending the soul'.

Such a *raison d'être* has never been associated with the Western magician, and herein lies a basic difference between the two traditions. Another is the absence in the shamanic tradition of any written material, and also the exclusion of any approach that could be described as 'intellectual'. This *blending* of the right and left brain (to use a modern concept) that is so important in the Western Tradition is totally absent.

The comments of Jung are particularly relevant here as they support the shamanic view.

> Rationality is only one aspect of the world and does not cover the whole field of experience. Psychic events are not caused merely from within and mental contents are not mere derivatives of sense-perceptions.[74]

This principle, when applied to the shaman, would be taken to mean that he or she lives almost exclusively in the 'supernatural dimensions'.

The magical powers attributed to the shaman (and both men and women are practitioners) are similar to those claimed by the *yogis* of the third century AD – those phenomena known as *siddhis*. Here, mastery of the mind gives the practitioner various enviable skills – to fly, walk on water, become invisible, have knowledge of past and future, enter the minds of others and understand the language of animals. These attributes are referred to as sorcery or – particularly in reference to Merlin who had mastered them all – wizardry.

Shamanism originated in Siberia, had its origins in the Neolithic period, and pre-dates all organised religion. Of its etymological origins, *Tungus* – the relevant linguistic term – translates as 'one who knows'. Another definition, perhaps more evocative of shamanic practices, is 'they who walk in the sky'. The practice later became an intrinsic part of Tibetan Buddhism, as the shamanic peoples of Tibet found that faith to their liking. The practice seems to suit not obviously welcoming places such as deserts, and much is made of wild creatures, rocks and shrubs as being totemic.

To the shaman, an association with animal spirits is paramount; that and a profound link with the land. The power that is utilized by the shaman is that of the cosmos, but specifically natural forces such as the wind and lightning. The problem for the modern shaman is that the Earth has been so ravaged and perverted in urban society. He or she is forced to practice their art in isolated places, those that still preserve some of their original potency.

This equality intrinsic to shamanism may have attracted Madame Blavatsky, later the founder of the Theosophical Society, when she was a young girl. Helena Blavatsky sought out the acquaintance of Baranig Boyrak, an old sage who lived near her grandparents' home. She wished

---

74 Jung, *ibid.*, p.462

him to teach her the language of insects, birds and animals. Blavatsky later journeyed into the Caucasus, those parts of Georgia known in those days as Imeretia and Mingrelia, spending time in the company of other shamans, wizards and soothsayers. Her own class could not comprehend why the daughter of a colonel would prefer 'smoky huts' to 'brilliant drawing rooms'!

Shamanic Practice

The shaman's drum is a very important part of his magical armoury. The rhythmic beat created induces a dream-like state that enables the shaman to travel across the 'rainbow bridge' into one or even two spirit worlds. These are the upper and lower worlds, which have very distinctive characteristics. The images associated with the former are 'climbing a mountain, tree, cliff, rainbow, or ladder; ascending into the sky on smoke; flying on an animal'. The lower world is associated with 'entering into the earth through a cave, hollow tree stump, a water hole, a tunnel or tube.[75]

The shaman, as well as being respected, is also feared for his ability to cause harm to others if he so wishes. The 'black' shaman takes his power from the direction of the North and is considered to be most powerful because he is a warrior shaman. Through his courage and strength he has the ability to overcome evil. Although he practices healing, the giving of protection and divination, he is quite capable of putting curses on his enemies.

The 'white' shaman takes his power from the west and uses it to pacify angry spirits. He is at one with the spirits of nature, and is altogether more benign in his approach. This distinct division of the two kinds of magic is another factor in separating the shamanic tradition from its Western counterpart.

The Native American tradition of 'shamanism' cannot strictly speaking be described in this way, as it is historically so diverse. The culture boasts healers, ritualists, mystics and medicine men, but none of

---

75 'The Caves of Pluto' fulfils this definition perfectly. Situated in desert lands to the north of Mt. Shasta, California, these extraordinarily extensive underground chambers are resonant of the shamanic world. Photographs of the caves, and other sacred sites in the USA, may be found on my website: www.gordonstrong.co.uk

the people themselves describe themselves as 'shamans'. Any similarity in methods of spiritual practice is almost coincidental.

The practices of the Navajo tribe have been perhaps the most accessible to those researching the Native American culture. As the American government, through its military aggression, sought to entirely destroy this culture in the late nineteenth century, it is distinctly ironic that anthropologists have in recent times been so eager to investigate it.

The American landscape, majestic and magnificent as it is, evokes a feeling of timelessness and eternity. The area of the Painted Hills in Eastern Oregon has an almost indescribable quality, its beauty and vibrancy almost overwhelming to the traveller who tunes in to its sacred resonance. It is one of the great tragedies of history that the American people themselves, the former white settlers, so often regard their own wonderful land and its authentic culture with such indifference.

Carlos Castaneda

Carlos Castaneda was an anthropologist at the University of California in Los Angeles in the 1960s. His first three published works were originally written as research theses. These books, *The Teaching of Don Juan, A Separate Reality,* and *Journey to Ixtlan* detail the philosophy of Don Juan, a Yaqui sorcerer. Don Juan describes the world as 'stupendous, awesome, mysterious, unfathomable'.[76] He also mentions various attributes that the 'warrior's way' must encompass – 'personal power', 'impeccability', and 'controlled folly'.

In his later writings Castaneda mentions the Toltec, or Tolteca, assigning them the role of 'sorcerers of Ancient Mexico'. This may be an idiosyncratic definition of their culture, as it is one which other anthropologists have found difficult to isolate or define. It is still impressive that to the Toltec civilization is attributed the art of healing, calendars, and sacred wisdom.

To dismiss Castaneda's writings as works of fiction, as some have done, is not only extremely short-sighted but ridiculous. Those who take this view entirely miss the point. The philosophy that Castaneda presents, in such a compelling and dramatic format, is one of awe-

---

76 Carlos Castaneda, *A Journey to Ixtlan* (London: The Bodley Head, 1972)

inspiring wisdom. He is to be congratulated not reviled for his efforts, and one can only encourage students to read his early works.

Being first published in 1969, Castaneda's work was often associated with the hippie and drug culture of that period. In fact it is only in the first volume, *The Teachings of Don Juan*, that peyote and jimson weed are mentioned. Peyote, a psychoactive plant (the use of which dates back to 4000 BC), supposedly instils feelings of insight and euphoria in those who ingest it. Jimson weed (loco weed) is a Chinese medicine that has healing properties, though by ingesting the plant Don Juan's pupil is reduced to a condition where he cannot distinguish reality and fantasy. It does not need to be mentioned more than once (and for reasons that are self-explanatory) that drugs, including alcohol, have no place whatsoever in the Western Magical Tradition.

The Theory of Ritual Magic

Rituals are not the path; they are the reminder that there is a path.

Judith Stanton

What is a ritual? The response could be, 'a design, a formal pattern, and one with intention'. It is also a dramatic production, but one performed without the slightest intention of impressing an audience. Evelyn Waugh, recounting his memories of a Catholic Mass, uses terms appropriate to our thesis.

> When I first came into the Church I was drawn, not by splendid ceremonies but by the spectacle of the priest as a craftsman. He had an important job to do which none but he was qualified for. He and his apprentice stumped up to the altar with their tools and set to work without a glance to those behind them, still less with any intention to make a personal impression on them.[77]

What makes the performance 'magical' is the intention to invoke the spiritual realm. The magician, dependent upon the means at his disposal and how well-honed his expertise may be, creates his own world about him. The Will and the Imagination combine to produce magic – the imagination creates an image, and the will manifests it upon the conscious plane. Mike Harris talks of 'a conduit for inner power to have credence in the physical world.'[78] During a ritual the sacred space created is the mental sphere where magic takes place.

---

77 Michael Davie (ed.), *The Diaries of Evelyn Waugh 1911-1965* (London: Penguin, 1984) p.793
78 Harris, p.78

This is a fundamental principle of magic and why its practice requires total and utter conviction as to what is being done and where it is being carried out. This principle applies not only during ritual but away from it. One should not confuse 'dedication' with heaviness or pedantry, and indeed the magician must be able to 'switch off' his powers. The magical calling, however, is never 'part-time' or trivial.

A degree of drama is always present in a ritual, and this must be so. The 'artistic temperament' as it is described (often pejoratively) is always present in the magician. He is often a curious mixture of the scientist and the artist. At once detached, and at the same time fully aware of the potential and profundity of the forces that he engages. Jung speaks of art and the creative individual in terms that we can recognise as referring to magic and the magician.

> ...it rises far beyond the personal, speaking from and for the spirit and heart of humanity... Every creative person is a duality or a synthesis of paradoxical qualities. On the one hand he is human and personal, but on the other an impersonal, creative process... Art is innate in him as a driving force which takes hold of him and makes him its instrument... As a person he may have moods and wishes and his own aims, but as an artist he is 'human' in a higher sense, he is a collective person, a carrier and former of the unconsciously active psyche of humanity.[79]

It should be noted that there is a great difference between *invocation* and *evocation*. The former seeks to create within the magician's consciousness the aetheric energies that are outside him. Crowley describes *devotion*, *identification* and *drama* as three separate approaches to invocation. He also describes the state of mind that is desirable for the task.

> The mind must be exalted until it loses consciousness of self. The Magician must be carried forward blindly by a force which, though in him and of him, is by no means that which he in his normal state of consciousness calls I. Just as the poet, the lover, the artist, is carried out of himself in a creative frenzy, so must it be for the Magician.[80]

Evocation seeks to create a tangible form from the inner energies, hence the use of incense to provide a medium. The magic detailed in the

---

79   Jung, *ibid.*, p.477
80   Crowley, *ibid.*, p.97

medieval *grimoires*[81] is generally concerned with methods to call forth demons and command them. Only the most experienced of magicians ever attempt evocation, and even such a celebrated occultist as Eliphas Levi did not recommend the practice.

As one might expect, the most fortuitous time for a ritual is determined by the Moon and the season. Our ancestors knew this only too well and ordered their lives accordingly. Every full moon has its own particular energy, and this variation in character should be assiduously studied. It is not the operator however, but the Divine Plan that determines whether any magical undertaking will succeed. Human will has achieved extraordinary feats, but ultimately the same impetus that brought the universe into existence will determine how it is shaped and how (and if!) it will continue.

Magicians, as individuals, differ greatly in temperament, thus what *appeals* to the initiate is important. He should follow only what is clearly relevant to himself and that which serves his purpose. We may mention certain advice given by a schoolmaster as to the writing of poetry:

> Once you secure the right to pass over anything, read or said, as of no meaning for your present purposes, you have the foundation for real easy creativeness.[82]

The magician strives to attain a state of mind that embodies his calling, but he should not be a mere shadow of those whose teachings he follows. Whatever strikes a magical chord – he should use or adapt to his own methods. It is *the individual's* working, no one else has any say in that magical world apart from the Masters, and they will soon inform the magus if they disapprove of anything he does.

Crowley was referring to the unique quality of the individual when he said "Do what *thou* wilt"[83]. Only through the self can one act, no one else can do it. Help the cause, and gain strength and wisdom by performing selfless and noble acts. Seek out angels and gods as companions; they will soon uncannily appear. Work with the most powerful magic that it is possible to muster. Aim for the highest and be rewarded accordingly.

---

81 The word is derived from 'grammar', literally the mechanics of the medium.
82 G.Y.Elton, *Teaching English* (London: Macmillan, 1934) p.12
83 Perhaps the most misinterpreted and abused dictum in the history of magic.

It is within ourselves that the truth lies; thus the magician must know what is required of him. Dion Fortune describes this duty as being:

> ...characterized by two things, the power to be still and wait, and the power to stand absolutely alone. Until we know how to be still, mentally as well as physically, we cannot handle power; ...the initiate is prepared to work without seeing result, playing his part on the Great Plan that unfolds through the ages of planetary time. [84]

The magician walks diligently upon his ordained path and does not stray from it. The ways of the magician are hidden from the eyes of others. Magicians are rarely social creatures, for by walking a lone path the magus preserves his power, and does not dissipate it in the outside world.

Man may be more divine than angels simply because he has the power to create, something which angels cannot do. Angels obey commands, they do not originate actions. So in doing magic, man becomes as a deity. Assuming the character of a god will achieve the purpose of the ritual much more quickly and effectively.

Truth and Illusion

The objective world is composed of form; the subjective is reliant upon some *meaning* in order to exist. Since the time of Hume and Berkeley it has been the ambition of philosophers to establish that an *objective reality* exists. From the moment that Einstein questioned Newton's absolutist theory of the forces that shaped the universe, the question became the province of science. It is perhaps not so extraordinary that metaphysics and physics are now often seen to be holding hands and walking in the same direction.

It is as well to remember that nothing is as it appears to be. As Castaneda tells us, our world,

> ...which we believe to be unique and absolute, is only one in a cluster of consecutive worlds, arranged like the layers of an onion...other realms which are as real, unique, absolute and engulfing as our own world is. [85]

---

84 Dion Fortune, *The Magical Battle of Britain*, Letter No.50 Nov.24th 1940 (Cheltenham: Skylight Press, 2012)
85 Castaneda, *ibid.*, p.108

The 'uncertainty principle' is at the heart of Quantum Probability and insists that there is no independence of perception or 'absolute reality' underlying existence. In his later career even such a great mind as Einstein valiantly attempted to prove that such a thing existed, but he did not succeed. Let practitioners of magic accept that those occultists they follow always knew that the universe was a phenomenal, not a causal one.

Not that such a debate precludes the notion of faith – once described as 'the substance of things hoped for'. Along with prayer, faith is an absolute, positive force. It is yet another example of the power of the human brain to invent, evaluate and achieve, the degree of which is quite extraordinary. A human brain is capable of making more synaptic connections than there are stars in the heavens. Its capacity for delighting us with wit and creations of sublime beauty is also amazing.

We dream, and our dreams have no prior intention of deceiving, they simply tell the tale as best they can. They belong to the realm of the unconscious, where our actions are determined far more than we realise. We must also never allow our conscious thoughts to dominate us. Thought is, like fire, a good servant but a bad master. As Nietzsche stated[86] – 'thoughts exist independent of our being, we do not will them into action.' They circle about us like starlings, often diverting in the way they twist and turn in flight, but the great bulk of them are meaningless and irrelevant to our existence. They are almost always of no value to our magical progress.

If the laws of physics were suddenly reversed or removed, the conscious world would appear as the unconscious. On the Inner planes it is the magician who sets the rules of the game. The magician is not subject to any limitation of Time or Space, and therefore, in having mastery of the moment, he can decide absolutely the nature of that moment.

Hermetic Magic

The Caduceus is a wand, about which is entwined two serpents. Their heads are turned to face each other – a symbol of peace and

---

86 In the original German: "*ein Gedanke kommt, wenn 'er' will, und nicht wenn 'ich' will*"

reconciliation. At the upper end of this 'staff' there are two wings, representing the speed of thought, and the notion of 'mind over matter'. This was Apollo's gift to Mercury (Hermes) in exchange for the lyre which he had invented. The Caduceus has the power to answer any question, and resolve every dispute in the world. On this principle is Hermetic Magic founded.

The wisdom of Hermes and the 'Universal Life' is personified as a dragon – named 'Hermes' in some versions of the legend. The dragon represents the paradox of magic in that the true nature of wisdom is concealed behind the awesome and fearful appearance of the dragon. In the ancient Mystery Schools this metamorphosis was depicted in dramatic form. A neophyte, if deemed ready to encounter the Mysteries, would encounter such an extraordinary experience as the following is described.

> The aged initiator, raising his wand, cried out in a loud voice: 'All hail Thee, Thoth Hermes, Thrice Greatest; all hail Thee, Prince of Men; all hail Thee who standeth upon the head of Typhon!' At the same instant a lurid writhing dragon appeared – a hideous monster, part serpent, part crocodile, and part hog. From its mouth and nostrils poured sheets of flame, and horrible sounds echoed through the vaulted chambers. Suddenly Hermes struck the advancing reptile with the serpent-wound staff and, with a snarling cry, the dragon fell over upon its side, while the flames about it slowly died away. Hermes placed his foot upon the skull of the vanquished Typhon. The next instant, with a blaze of unbearable glory that sent the neophyte staggering backward against a pillar, the immortal Hermes, followed by streamers of greenish mist, passed through the chamber and faded into nothingness.[87]

The intention is that such a revelation forces the student to observe a spectacle that is impossible to explain. He must be prepared to accept what he has experienced as a true depiction of the nature of magic. The way of magic is a series of inexplicable encounters, crises of spirit and mind-altering experiences. The great lesson is that there is a need to acquire a balanced temperament in order to cope with the vagaries of existence. Only when this is achieved can the student expect to deal with the magical happenings that he will experience, inevitably far beyond anything that he could have ever imagined.

---

87 *The Life and Teachings of Thoth Hermes Trismegistus*, www.sacred-texts.com

One of the most important attributes of the magician is that of concentration. Without acquiring this skill he will be lost and subsequently in a very vulnerable state. The 'purpose' of magic will be discussed in detail later in our study, for now we must establish the most effective method of achieving our ends.

By absolutely focusing his intention, the magician ensures that his magic is operating at the greatest intensity and the highest degree of power. If he loses that focus the force wanes to nothing and he may as well cease all magical activities until he is in a more fit state to proceed. A simple thing such as tiredness can bring about this sense of languor, so the magician should constantly be aware of his mental and physical state.

It is essential also that the magician continually reviews his methods and motives. The current of energy in any place of magical working will vary as much as there are vagaries in the English weather. For this reason it is absolutely essential to maintain a high level of 'magical consciousness' in the place of working. This is achieved through respect and dedication to ritual, the powers invoked, and the physical aspect of the Temple. A rigorous approach will altogether ease the entry of the divine current in whatever way the practitioner uses to bring this about.

The 'slings and arrows' of life are unavoidable, but ill-fortune should never deter the magician from his calling. If it does then he should surrender his right to the title of 'magus' forthwith. A faith in magic must be absolute, only then it will see us through any 'sea of troubles'. It is this initial belief in magic that brought us to the mysteries, so let us never lose sight of the strength and purity of that original impetus.

Correspondences

Using 'correspondences' is the practice of employing certain associations for magical purposes.[88] It is a procedure that the student should study and employ as soon as he is able. This was the way of the ancients, and in the realm of practical magic it has yet to be bettered. By discovering the links between objects and ideas, we begin to construct our own

---

88 Alan Richardson, *The Magician's Tables: A Complete Book of Correspondences* (London: Godsfield Press, 2007).

universe. Because we have ordered it ourselves, we have dominion over it. This is yet another principle of magic.

> The whole natural world corresponds to the spiritual world – not just the natural world in general, but actually in details. So anything in the natural world that occurs from the spiritual world is called a correspondent. It is vital to understand that the natural world emerges and endures from the spiritual world, just like an effect from the cause that produces it.[89]

The Magician realizes that everything that happens around him is particular to his own rapport with the universe. To take this awareness one step further, he employs magical communication to inform the universe of his intentions. Similarly, when he is himself being informed of some aspect of the universe he is in a state of meditation. Magical correspondences aid the student, not only by building a magical language, but also by constructing a magical picture for him.

Swiftness of thought and, more importantly, speed of perception are what sets the magician apart from his fellows. As we have seen, the magician trains himself to perceive the true essence of all things. Thus he knows the whereabouts of the gates of power, those points where access to the other world is most easily gained.

The Celts believed that where two elements met was the place where the veil was at its most thin. These were: at dusk – between light and dark; on the shore – earth and water; and at the top of mountains where air and earth connect.

For the student, an invaluable exercise is to compile planetary correspondences – the colours, gems and metals that are associated with a particular planet. For example the planet Mars has a correspondence with iron, fire, soldiery, surgery, thorn, onions, chili, the colour crimson, etc. All living things too have astrological correspondences, and for those who wish to study the lore of plants *Culpeper's Herbal* is an excellent reference work. Placing elements that are in harmony with the theme of the ritual – incense, images and objects – all will increase the chance of its success.

---

89 Emanuel Swedenborg, *The True Christian Religion* (Stockholm: Swedenborg Society, 1890)

The Ways of the Magician

Blaise Pascal in the renowned *Pensées*, was almost triumphant in his regarding of man's intellectual impotence in the presence of the cosmos.

> For after all what is man in nature? A nothing in relation to infinity, all in relation to nothing, a central point between nothing and all, and infinitely far from understanding either. The ends of things and their beginnings are impregnably concealed from him in an impenetrable secret. He is equally incapable of seeing the nothingness out of which he was drawn and the infinite in which he is engulfed.[90]

Speculating upon the nature of God is an exercise inevitably undertaken by the philosopher. The late Lawrence Gardner questioned the notion that there was ever a supreme deity at all, preferring to suggest that Jehovah was an invention of the Israelite scribes. To Gardner, God had never been a historical constant, just a theme developed over a considerable period of time by different cultures.

The nature of Christ is an idea more easily embraced by the magical practitioner. The Messiah *(the annointed)* represents light, sacrifice and, through healing, the ultimate good. These qualities are, or definitely should be, part of magical theory and practice. The essence of mystery that surrounds Christ's presence is lyrically evoked by Stephen Medcalf:

> ...to look into Jesus's imagination is like looking into the sun. It is difficult to see what is at work there, virtually impossible to think of questioning it, but its power is overwhelming...[91]

Such sentiments are completely in harmony with the Western Magical Tradition.

The magician is concerned with the nature of heaven as it is the source of his power. He would be as hesitant in giving it a physical location as the Oxford English Dictionary is cautious in its definition – suggesting 'abode of God' and 'place or state of bliss'. The magician cannot similarly afford to hedge his bets; he must come to terms with the source of the divine light that he experiences.

---

90 Blaise Pascal, *Pensées*, Number 72.
91 Brian Cummings, Gabriel Josipovici (eds) *The Spirit of England: selected essays by Stephen Medcalf* (Oxford: Oxbow Books, 2010) p.210.

Dion Fortune speaks of the 'riches of the higher mind', and certainly the aim of the magician should be to set his sights on attaining the realm of the super-conscious. The magician strives as much as possible to be part of this *Universal Mind*. He understands that:

> ...our thoughts generate the physical world just as God is said to have used the power of thought to generate the light and sound that manifested as the Universe. [92]

Naturally, it is easier to allow oneself to be enveloped in the *universal consciousness* – the material world with all its illusions and emptiness. It is almost as if those who are trapped in this plane are ignorant of their actual existence. They are not to be wholly condemned – more pitied. The manner in which an individual's soul is consciously manifest during their span on Earth bears no relation to the 'higher self' that each one of us own. This aspect of their essence is beyond any attachment to the physical plane. If the magician is truly at one with the universe then nothing within it can ever have any effect upon him, let alone ever harming him. If Love is united with Power, the magician will be the friend of all and the enemy of none. The magician, like Don Juan's warrior, should always appear to be without fear.

Motive is all in magic, and *belief* in success is the key to any practical results. If a ritual is conducted with the correct intention, and with due devotion and respect, it is more likely that it will reap great rewards. The purpose of magic is to bring light into the world, and if a ritual achieves this end then all to the good. Those who involve themselves in 'chaos magic', the 'left-hand path' and other pitiful aberrations of true magic deserve the consequences, and without doubt they will bring ill-fortune upon themselves. Such is the nature of the True Light – it may blind those who wallow in darkness.

---

92 Da Silva, *The Mind and Myth* (Hampton Roads: Charlottesville Virginia, 2002) p.298

8

Practical Magic

Yield yourself utterly to the Will of Heaven, and you become the omnipotent instrument of that Will.

Aleister Crowley

A s our thesis has suggested, there is little to be gained in occult practice from *restricting* oneself to theory – this is the way of 'armchair magic'. A magician must be active and forthright, hence his affinity with Don Juan's warrior. Merlin gains much from his association with King Arthur and vice-versa. The universe needs the magician, to circulate its power and to bring light and energy into every corner of its infinite domain. The magician is a hero, a god, and a force for all that is fine – it is a noble calling.

> The nature of a constitution, the action of an assembly, the play of parties, the unseen formation of a guiding opinion, are complex facts, difficult to know and easy to mistake. But the action of a single will, the fiat of a single mind, are easy ideas: anybody can make them out, and no one can ever forget them.[93]

Thoth is the Egyptian god of Magic and Writing and for good reason. Both callings require one to be alone; a place from where the greatest strength is gained. If an individual is not at ease with his own company, how can he possibly be so with others?

In his own role the magician is akin to the artist, the actor and even the stand-up comic. One of the most profound lessons of the Fool is 'never to take oneself seriously'. That is why the two Tarot cards of The

---

93 Walter Bagehot, *The English Constitution* (London: Collins, 1963) p.82

Magician and The Fool make such a splendid pair – one still, one in constant animation.

The very existence of any individual depends upon the willingness of the cosmos to bestow upon them the precious gift of life. The magician is an agent of that same Cosmos – a 'special agent' perhaps! And of what is man a manifestation? He is of the heavens, the universe and all within them – a parade of masques, a bundle of energies, a composite of impressions. He exists but does not – a synthesis of different energies – a cocktail of atoms!

At all times, the magician should never be in any doubt as to the origin of the power that he employs. The material that makes up the physical form is owned by none. Every atom in our bodies has seen service in another form, and at another time. All is in a state of constant change and must be so, for change is energy.

Pure matter is matter in motion, for it cannot be permitted to be inert. All that enters the heart of the magician must be purified, by removing any falsity or negative influences. The essence must be cleansed so that the divine attracts the divine. Sacrifice is the acknowledgement of this law – the surrender of the mundane personality to be replaced by the magical version.

Preparing for Magic

The period before the New Moon, and also before the Spring Equinox are known for their uncertain, even volatile energies. The flow of the *Tattwic Tides*, as they are referred to, must also be taken into consideration. This determines that particular energies appear at certain times of the year – Fire in the Spring, Water in the Summer, Air in the Autumn, and Earth in the Winter. Some practitioners will do no magical work between the Vernal and the Spring Equinox, maintaining that the earth needs this six month period to regain its energy. The denizens of the animal kingdom remain dormant, and it is known that many humans suffer from a lack of energy in this period.

Correct preparation for ritual is essential. The magical personality must be assumed. In order to do this, the practitioner studies his face in a mirror to establish that what he sees is only an illusion. He then replaces this image with one of magical significance. This may be a god form, or whatever he chooses it to be.

Establishing a magical name and referring to oneself by that title enhances personal power. The name must be revealed to no one, for it is the magician's personal key to the Astral Planes. When magical organisations were more prevalent, a lodge name was used with fellow members, a private name outside in the world. It is important for the magician to distance himself from his calling, not during ritual when he should be totally involved in what he is doing, but with regard to strangers and any others he may encounter.

When deciding upon a magical name which suits the character of the individual personality, Bill Gray suggests asking these questions:

Who am I?
What am I?
Where am I?

The chosen name should then be meditated upon to ensure that it has the approval of the Masters of the Inner Planes.

Gray also insists that every gesture made in the Temple is most significant. He stresses the importance of approaching the altar with appropriate body movements, pertinent to the nature of the ritual. Gray's approach is part of a philosophy that stresses the importance of *all* things, even those that appear to be unimportant.

We delude ourselves if we believe that we are ever fully in control of the state that we perceive as 'reality'. The most apparently foolproof scheme never is, as many have discovered! The foregone conclusion does not exist. As Dion Fortune reminds us:

We live in the midst of invisible forces whose effects alone we perceive. We move among invisible forms whose actions we very often do not perceive at all, though we may be profoundly affected by them.[94]

Magical Weapons

The traditional term 'magical weapons' may perhaps give an incorrect impression of these essential items. 'Tools' would perhaps be a better

---

94 Dion Fortune, *Aspects of Occultism* (Wellingborough, Aquarian Press, 1962) p.78

description. These are four artefacts used by the magician during ritual. Each has its own purpose and associations, many of which are given here. The student would be well advised to seek out others. It may be helpful to consider Wands as 'edges', Swords as 'points', Cups as 'carriers', and Pentacles as 'surfaces'.

The Wand represents Fire and the Will, though it should be noted that the human will is powerless against the hand of God. Mars, like any other planet, is subject to the solar light, and its illumination is greater. The wand is a symbol of strength, aid and intention. It also represents prevention, banishment and invocation. It can be seen that all the magical weapons have a dual purpose. The wand may *prevent entry* by being held horizontally, and it may give *freedom of passage* when held upright by the practitioner.

The wand is a conductor and an indicator, and is used when creating a boundary circle during ritual – clockwise to consecrate, anti-clockwise to deconsecrate. This circular motion with the wand may be likened to a spiral staircase, in that it draws power upwards and downwards and is also capable of creating a ladder to the heavens. The wand indicates motion back and forth yet its rule is firm, so that any movement is always deliberate and made with the utmost resolve.

The Sword represents Air – a symbol of wisdom. The dawn, Spring, the feathered arrow – like a bird – all these give the impression of travel and movement. Speed of thought is obviously included. Breath is life, and the sword may be used as a scalpel – to heal by cutting and penetration. The sword is taken from the scabbard and used to salute the higher powers, acknowledging the magician's obedience to them. It also compels obedience and may defend or wound others. Its intention is sure and it may be as the scythe, harvesting that which sustains us – the corn for the bread of life – or cutting away that which is no longer necessary. The archetypal depiction of Death has him carrying a scythe.

The hilt of a magical sword must be of copper (the metal governed by Venus) so that it balances the iron of Mars. This is yet another meeting of god and goddess and, without such a union the sword is worthless as a magical artefact. A sword made solely of steel has only *the will* to guide it, and thus may be used for good or ill. The implication is that the sword must be guided only by means of divine power.

As Jupiter, Venus is regarded by astrologers as being a beneficent planet. At her highest vibration she radiates goodness and beauty and so has the power to be transmuted into the sword of truth, for as the poet would have us believe, 'beauty is truth'.

The Cup contains, it is the form-giver – the womb, the well. It is also the *carrier* of consciousness – moving between heaven and earth. The cup cleanses and purifies. The sun draws up water from the Earth into the air to fall again in a continual cycle of filling and emptying. The cup is also the lamp, lighting the way into other dimensions and experiences. It brings life from death and expresses emotion – predominantly love. It is also a sign of communion in the widest sense, for its vibration is within the unifying power of music which moves us to express our joy. With the sense of hearing, we acknowledge the way others communicate to us.

The Pentacle is the shell or the platter, but it may also be the shield of protection – the roof over our heads. It is gravity, stillness, wholeness and place. When the Earth is benign, its beauty and fruits sustain us; when it is in motion in the form of an earthquake it disturbs us in its terror. Earth cannot be regarded as solid; its supposed permanence is an illusion.

The *field* in which we work, either mentally or physically is held by the Pentacle, for it is the 'outside' while the Cup is the interior. It is knowledge, and hopefully wisdom. Its ability to protect is demonstrated by the heraldic devices upon a shield, inscribed there to ward off unwanted energies.

Ritual Methods

The purpose of detailing various practices here is not with the aim of insisting upon rigid rules of magical procedure, but to inspire and to suggest. It does however seem a sensible rule to establish a basic framework for ritual work. One should not, of course, be a slave to *form*. The Magus should learn to take things in his stride. Arriving for a ritual and discovering a wand has been inadvertently left behind, or a script lost, means but little in the great magical scheme!

Improvisation is the name of the game! A wand can just as easily be a finger pointed in the right direction – a chalice a pair of cupped hands. What is important is *being there in that place at that moment and doing magic*. Being anxious or po-faced is anathema to vitality and spontaneity. Once confidence is gained, the student should try speaking *extempore* – he will be amazed at how the magical words will flow, and his natural gestures suddenly adopt great power.

Every student would be well advised to consult the detailed instructions for the *Banishing Ritual of the Pentagram*[95]. All *traditional* magical operations are based upon this ritual, and others are really only variations upon it. Familiarising yourself with what is involved in this operation is an excellent exercise, not only for the magical memory but for simple concentration. To its advantage also is that the ritual may be successfully performed alone. The purpose of the *Banishing Ritual*, if it is performed before a main ritual, is to ensure that a pure and positive atmosphere permeates the scene of operations.

How a ritual begins sets the tone for the subsequent proceedings. Put the feet comfortably apart and stretch the arms out and above the head with the fingers pointed upward. Slowly bring the hands down by the sides. An awareness of the etheric field around the body may be felt.

It is important to recognise the significance of the direction East. The magician stands in the East, opposite the Priestess in the West. An altar in a church is always in the East, the sacred space beyond the chancel. The English clergy were adamant about this when cathedrals were built in Europe during the fourteenth century. There is of course 'magical east': any direction that the magician chooses. Thus one of our primary rules may be broken!

The opening of the four directions is the first procedure in a ritual, and one that should be carried out with a purposeful air. This is the initial contact with the divinities, and the practitioner should always show a proper respect for their authority. The four archangels may be invoked – they are invaluable allies. They are constant, reliable forces, mainly because they have been employed in magic for many hundreds of years. Their presence and images are easily contacted and always potent.

The order of opening the gates, or directions, is as follows: East – the element of Air, South – Fire, West – Water and North – Earth. The following invocation[96] of the four elements may be used.

---

95 A simplified version of this ritual can be found in Alan Richardson's *Magical Gateways,* p.55

96 This is my own composition, and I willingly give permission for any serious student to employ it.

May the wind of debate and justice circulate in the minds of men.
Let the fire of inspiration and all creative power shine upon the world.
May the waters of love, compassion and mercy flow freely into the heart of
every one of us.
Let the Earth be blessed and bring forth all goodness in every living thing.

As has already been mentioned, the Egyptian god forms are also eminently suitable for magical work. Thoth, Ra, Isis and Geb are the equivalent gates. Another variation is the sacred Celtic creatures, the Hawk of Dawn, the Rutting Stag, the Salmon of Wisdom and the Bear. Whichever pantheon is chosen must be adhered to, do not be tempted to mix and match.

The practitioner should also be aware that there are strictly speaking *Seven* directions. East, South, West and North – also *Above* and *Below* and *the Spirit* in the Centre. The Star of David – the union of Fire and Water – may also be considered as a symbol to be invoked above the place of magical working.

The area is then consecrated with fire and water by walking in a *deosil* (clockwise) direction about the central point (the altar). This means a slow procession with a lighted candle/incense to represent fire. Next, a few drops from a chalice are distributed at intervals during the circuit. This creating of a sacred space is most important. If engaged upon any temple business it is always good practice to walk about the altar in a deosil direction. This maintains the correct current of energy in this most sacred space.

Processing around the Temple three times with wand raised will also increase the energy. This being done, the magus states clearly who he is, thus announcing his presence to the powers, and the purpose of the ritual. After that, the presentation of offerings, those things that it is wished be manifested, and a meditation follow. The magician's third eye will open if the energy is high. Auras may be seen and the energy felt will be almost tangible, like the sensation of leaning into the wind. The potency of the ritual will depend upon the conviction of the sentiments expressed. Some advice on the writing of rituals is given elsewhere.

At the end of the ritual, deconsecrate the area, while walking *widdershins* (anti-clockwise). Close the four quarters in the opposite order they have been opened and announce that the ritual has ended by clapping the hands loudly once or twice. Some practitioners stamp upon the floor of the temple ten times to banish any unwanted entities. This final pronouncement indicates a return from the Inner Planes back to the mundane world. The transition from one type of awareness to another may not appear to be dramatic at the time, but experienced magicians will assure you that it is.

If the operator wishes to conduct rituals indoors on a regular basis, and the means are available to him, an actual temple space can be constructed.[97] For temple work, the Priestess should enter this space some time before the ritual begins and meditate in silence for some minutes. This exercise 'sets the astral juices flowing'.

Writing Rituals

Once the practitioner has decided upon the theme of a ritual he wishes to do, he should attempt to set it down in writing. One's own version of a ritual is by definition the most personal, and writing rituals is excellent magical practice. Remember, it is not an academic treatise, more like composing poetry. Include the correct magical correspondences certainly, but then let the words flow – write from the heart and the imagination. The more the writer really means the words that have been written, the greater the effect achieved when the ritual is performed. Experiment too with intoning words with your lips closed and producing the deepest vibration possible. This technique was known in the Middle Ages as the way of 'wizards that peep and mutter'.

The challenge is to give voice to sentiments which are often beyond mere words. The power of speech is often not assigned the importance that it deserves. The roots of language lie in ancient sacred practice rather than secular convenience. As Curtius tells us:

> The assertion that the oldest words presuppose some relation between sounds and the representation they designate has often been ridiculed. It is difficult, however, to explain the origin of language without such assumptions.[98]

---

97 Invaluable information on this aspect of magical practice can be found in Gareth Knight, *Magical Images and the Magical Imagination* (Oceanside, USA: Sun Chalice, 1999) p.55

98 Percy Walker, *The Message in the Bottle* (New York: Farrar, Straus and Giroux, 1954) p.79

Another reason for writing a ritual is that the task of composition forces the magician to make a leap of the imagination. Like all writing, the words used in a ritual should be succinct. Composing pieces that are to be spoken aloud is a different exercise to simply writing prose to be read. The words must *resonate* with authority when they fill the temple – as all sound during a ritual. Words, provided they are given the correct weight, have the added advantage of making connections in the unconscious. The greatest magicians were also consummate *actors*, delivering each piece *dramatically*.

Pay attention to the *timbre* of the words used. The sentiment, 'Be together as one' has a sweeter ring than 'Transference', for instance. Let the words come, so that it is not the intellect that determines their choice but an inner urge to express something greater. The ancients knew only too well the power of words and the sounds they made. This is an aspect of magic that is often sorely neglected. Socrates, speaking of poetry, had this to say:

> …must know how to embody in sounds and syllables the name of each object which is naturally appropriate to it. Surely, if he is to be an authoritative name-giver, he must make up and bestow all his names with his eye fixed on the absolute or ideal name of what he is naming.

If rhythm and melody are present when words are spoken or sung they have tremendous power. Victorian hymns have this quality; the sentiments they express are stirring and memorable. When the magician extemporizes he is inspired by a spiritual force outside himself. As R.J.Stewart informs us,

> …this ritual pattern is shared between humans and other beings…humans and spiritual beings. You cannot have magic without the harmonious exchange between humanity and other orders of life. A ritual, a ceremony, is a special pattern that enables this exchange.[99]

The *universal* principle inherent in the ritual must always be kept in focus, whatever is being presented on a personal level. This is essential when writing ritual or the actual content may degenerate simply into wish-fulfilment. It should always be remembered that the role of the magician is as a *conductor of light*.

---

99 R.J.Stewart, *Ceremony and Ritual Magic* (New York: Harper Collins, 1990) p.162

Symbols and Talismans

Since the Middle Ages people have used magic squares, angelic signatures and Qabalistic signs to bring about good or evil designs. In the sixteenth century Paracelsus revived the talismanic tradition of consecrating certain metals with symbols. An amulet (Latin *amuletum*) should not be confused with a talisman (Greek *telesma)*. The former passively protects the owner (such as the Christian cross or the Eye of Horus), while the latter (as *Excalibur*) makes possible magical transformation. As William James tells us,

> Our normal waking consciousness ... is but one special type of consciousness, whilst all about it, parted from it by the flimsiest of screens, there lie potential forms of consciousness entirely different.[100]

Talismans are endowed with supernatural power, either by nature, or by being constructed in a ritualistic manner at particular hours of the day. Precious stones may be talismans as other objects. It is accepted amongst Hebrews that the Jewish prayer shawl, the *tallish*, has talismanic qualities, yet the Christian faith has always been wary of such objects.

Instructions to create a talisman can be found in many grimoires. The most commonly constructed is the Seal of Solomon. Catherine de Medici owned a talisman that depicted the god Jupiter, the eagle of Ganymede, Anubis and Venus. Both talismans and amulets occur in every civilization, and are particularly prevalent in Hindu and Buddhist culture.

The pentagram[101] is the most well-known magical symbol. It being depicted always as a *five* pointed star[102] is not necessarily correct. In the Middle Ages the term pentagram could also refer to the hexagram (Solomon's Seal). The word probably derives from the old French 'to hang' (as a pendant) thus by definition it is a talisman, and later a symbol used in magical operations.

The significance of the number five, however, is well-recorded. The five wits, the five fingers, the five wounds of Christ are well known, as also the five pure joys and the five virtues – generosity, fellowship,

---

100 William James, *Some Problems of Philosophy* (London: Penguin 1987) p.245
101 Also called *Pentacle, pentalpha, pentancle, pentangle or pentagle*.
102 The design is said to be based on the path made by the planet Venus in its
    conjunction with the sun.

purity, courtesy and mercy. The Hebrews ascribed five as the number of Truth and the Pentateuch, and the Greeks made the pentagram part of the golden ratio. This latter attribution may have been instrumental in the Romans using the pentagram as a symbol of the building trades. Later the Freemasons used it in their own regalia, though not in their rituals.

The notion that an inverted pentacle represents evil is extremely doubtful if not totally erroneous. Eliphas Levi considers it to be so but some of his deeply held assertions surprisingly turn out to be spurious. The other travesty is that, fuelled by the imagery adopted by 'heavy metal' bands, the association is now an established urban myth.

Sacred Sounds

Employing *all the senses* in a ritual adds other dimensions and thus gives the practitioner a broader canvas to work upon. Incense is well known as a medium for evocation, and colour and light are always employed for invocation. Sound is perhaps the least-used medium. It can be extremely powerful, as can words, but in a different way. Any tone, be it created by the resonance of the human voice or the use of bells, gongs and drums can be extremely effective.

The purpose of using sound is partly to raise the consciousness but, more importantly, to make contacts on the Inner Planes. If we wish to set up a line of communication with entities or deities appropriate to our working, this is the way to do it. It is the same when we wish to connect with natural forces – the spirit of the wind or water for instance. We must speak to these powers in their own language, attempting to reproduce the sounds that we hear.

Each of the cardinal directions has a tone associated with it, and the practice of using a note in the scale to stimulate a particular chakra has long been known. The Priest and Priestess chanting a duet or both using rhythmic patterns on drums can be very effective. Harmony and choir effects can be most effective with a group at a ritual, as can mixed percussion. With the latter exercise, by beginning slowly and increasing in speed, the corporate energy will be raised dramatically.

With communal efforts such as this it would be wise to appoint a ritual master. He has the task of sounding a gong when he feels that the performance has reached its peak. A period of silence after this outpouring of energy is also essential, probably as valuable as the exercise. The use of silence should never be overlooked – the absence of sound is as important as its presence.

Another way of working with sound is for the ritual master to produce a tone and then let the other members of the group attempt to approximate it. The *Om* sound is the most obvious choice. At Druidic ceremonies the *Arwen* is repeated three times using this method, and the climactic tone is held as long as possible.

W.G.Gray was convinced that the spiritual material needed for invocation could be compressed into a few tones. The sound produced would act as a 'call signal' – he describes the process as 'a pressure of consciousness'. Certainly a great intensity is experienced during a ritual if this practised. All taking part should be warned beforehand, as some people are simply too sensitive to endure these things.

The best method of producing vocal sounds according to Gray is to stand with legs together, right foot behind left. The arms should be extended, the palms upwards. If the sound is resonating fully, a feeling that the note is affecting the whole body should be experienced.

Gray's recommended magical technique is to *audibly* make the tone, and then *inaudibly* repeat it. This should be done as a thirty second exercise – fifteen seconds of making the tone and then a further fifteen seconds of producing that same sound silently. According to Gray, it is the second exercise which makes the connection with the Inner Planes.

Recordings are another available method of using sound, and abstract or formless music can be useful during meditation. It should never be intrusive, as some electronic effects can be overwhelming to those with sensitive hearing.

Darkest Hour

Through emanating the divine we become divine. The magician, when conducting a ritual may declare that he is a god, and only by wholeheartedly believing in the success of this transformation will he achieve anything approaching deity. This is a basic axiom of the Western Mystery Tradition. Naturally, there are pitfalls to this approach, as W.G.Gray warns.

...a danger exists of becoming 'God- intoxicated', suffering from Deistic delusions and the rest of such *Folie de Grandeur*...the history of religious mania is crammed with cases...where power is applied beyond an ability to deal with it...[103]

The testing of the initiate begins as soon as he ventures upon his path. If he '...finds that the circumstances of his life are beginning to blow up a storm, he will know that his application has been accepted...' [104] With regard to the Mysteries, a total freedom from ambition and self-interest is expected of the initiate. If he cannot relinquish these things then he is lost and will never walk upon the true path of magic, for it demands total commitment to an ideal. As Aleister Crowley insists, '...the greater thy trial the greater thy triumph.' If the initiate emerges from the fire redeemed, then he gains all.

It is the role of the Masters of the Inner Planes to aid the development of the seeker. Yet, they cannot permit the semi-enlightened or the impure to enter the sacred realm. It is necessary for all to experience an initiation where the emotions of terror and despair are their only companions. It is an experience that only the truly strong can pass through and gain the other side.

If we have no recognizable identity, then we may gain a new 'magical version' more easily. Without the burden of personality, the initiate gains an automatic empathy with all life on the earthly plane, thus he does not react adversely to any experience no matter how onerous. Perhaps this ideal state is akin to the nature of Melchizedek, 'Without father, without mother, without descent, having neither beginning of days, nor end of life'. The psychiatrist August Hoch describes:

> The stages of development into the new identity (which)...usually follow this pattern: crisis, interlude of apathy and dejection, followed by visions and dreams of death, possibly by drowning, the hearing of a command to take up a new identity, and finally a 'call' to reveal this new identity...

The *Watcher at the Gate* or *the Shadow* is often encountered in the beginning of the student's studies or even during his first magical ritual. In appearance this figure may resemble The Devil card in the Tarot. We must all come to terms with the darkness within us, and to deny this

---

103 W.G.Gray, *The Ladder of Lights*, (Cheltenham: Helios, 1968) p.45
104 Fortune, *ibid.*, p.87

aspect of ourselves is short-sighted and ultimately harmful. We should comfort ourselves by realizing that when we are drawn to such things as love, truth and beauty we are in harmony with the light. Thus we have made a choice and prefer not to wallow in the darkness of ignorance even though we must accept that it exists in the world.

The lesson we must learn from the 'Dweller on the Threshold' is one of identifying *hubris* or *spiritual pride* within ourselves. We must not be arrogant or superior as a result of acquiring knowledge. All of us who are engaged with magic are beholden to the masters to enlighten those who genuinely seek after knowledge. As Gareth Knight tells us:

> Those who work on the inner planes need help from us even as we need help from them, for the whole creation is joined together. No part is meant to work alone.[105]

By acknowledging that there are often conflicting aspects within us, we can begin to reconcile any conflict that we observe. We attract to ourselves that which is inside us. If we endeavour to maintain a state of harmony and inner peace then we are more likely to encounter a harmonious world. The magician must always try to retain a balanced personality. He must not allow any one of the four elements to become so prominent in his nature that it dominates the other three. As Crowley advises, referring to the spirits that reside within the elements:

> Be thou, therefore, prompt and active as the Sylphs, but avoid frivolity and caprice. Be energetic and strong as the Salamanders but avoid irritability and ferocity. Be flexible and attentive to images like the Undines, but avoid idleness and changeability. Be laborious and patient like the Gnomes, but avoid grossness and avarice. So shalt thou gradually develop the powers of thy soul, and fit thyself to command the spirits of the elements.[106]

These days, much talk is expounded on 'protection', most of which is unutterable nonsense. If we ask 'Protection from what?' we are likely only to receive a vague response, along the lines of 'harmful vibrations'. It is possible that anyone could be the victim of a psychic attack, but in practice very unlikely. Consider the hypothetical situation; why should

---

105 Knight, *ibid.*, p.282
106 Aleister Crowley, *The Confessions* (London: Penguin Arkana, 1987) p.220

some evil necromancer develop such hatred for an individual that nothing short of the devil possessing his soul will be adequate torment? This is the stuff of Dennis Wheatley novels.

It is more a case that the greatest fear is 'fear' itself, and the Magus should not embrace such an emotion. The only time he may have felt a frisson of terror was when he first encountered 'The Watcher at the Gate'. Then, his misgivings concerning magic and all that it meant were shown to be founded on his own imaginings. This is the moment when we discover whether our faith is as deep-rooted as we might like to believe.

If, as the Buddhist advocates, we should be 'in this world but not of this world', there is nothing there that can harm us because we are beyond its influence. When we are at a low ebb or under stress it is all too easy to imagine demons and monsters lurking in dark corners and ready to do us harm. We must banish these thoughts immediately and return once more to the replenishing light.

The rock on which we build our temple must be immovable, as must our dedication to the magical calling. Once we discover it has sand as its foundations, then we are lost. One thought, just a single idea can have the effect of dominating all our mental activity. This is not only dangerous, because it diverts our concentration, it is also debilitating of our intellectual and emotional energy. Obsession is a grave condition, one that can be seriously damaging to the individual. It could be said however, that an artist's total preoccupation with some theme in his work is beneficial. In this instance it promotes an intense attitude towards the work of art that might otherwise be absent.

9

Priest and Priestess

Courageous, untroubled, mocking, violent – that is what wisdom wants us to be: wisdom is a woman and loves only a warrior...

Nietzsche

Choosing suitable companions for the practice of magic is always a tricky business. Many are called but few are chosen. To join the Magus in his endeavours requires purity of intent and – it can never be stressed too often – *intent is all*. Egotists and curiosity seekers need not apply. The genuine seeker is marked by a humility and sincerity that touches the heart. Experiencing magical harmony with the like-minded is a rewarding experience, hence the awesome power created by the union of Priest and Priestess. A group of trusted companions will always make a ritual more powerful – the energy increases, the sum of the parts being greater than the whole.

With a group, the ritual becomes a 'ceremony'. It is essential that all those present respect the power of the symbols being used in the proceedings. They must also realize that things unseen are as important as those perceived. 'Occult' means 'hidden' and much that occurs will be unknown even to the magus, on occasion. All those who are taking part in a ritual must be aware that they are a medium for powers beyond the veil, forces that are frequently beyond the ken of man.

As we have learned, polarity is a very different concept to the insidious notion of duality. If magical workings are practised by the magician alone they may have every chance of success if the Divine Will permits that to happen. If the priest, however, works magic with a priestess then the power will increase more than twofold. The feminine principle adds the element of *natural imagination* to the working.

The term 'priest' is from the Greek word for *elder* but the origins of the word 'priestess' gives her only the status of 'helper'. She dances, sings and makes music to elevate the vibration of any ceremony. More accurately, she is guardian of the temple, and holds the secrets of emanations and changes, hence her role as an oracle. Alan Richardson describes her as:

> ...neither Mother nor Virgin, but functions mysteriously on the hidden side of things, with powers not understood in the present age. In this aspect she represents a factor not a person...all potent on the inner planes if inert on the physical. She works with neither the physical powers of the Mother, nor the spiritual powers of the Virgin, but with the magnetic powers of her office.[107]

The polarity of priest and priestess may be symbolized in two ideas, respectively Arthur and the Grail. More prosaically, the relationship between the Sun and Moon promotes this notion. The Sun emerges as constant, masculine, the Original Source of Mind and the Spirit from which all life emanates. The Moon is seen as a reflection of Mother Earth and the changeability of an internal nature.

According to the Chinese *Dao*, this intrinsic polarity fuels the workings of the universe. *Yang* is created by movement, and when this activity reaches its limit, all becomes still – the state of *Yin*. Stillness exists until there is a return to movement once more. Within a state of activity there resides the potential of tranquility, albeit at the end of a particular cycle, and it follows that stillness has within it the quality of movement. The individual power is the source of the other, producing and reproducing energy in an endless process. Both *belong* to each other, and therefore exist in harmony.

The meaning of the word 'moon' (Latin, *mensis – month)* indicates that this feature of the heavens was used by the ancients as a measure of time. The earliest calendars are calculated from the passage of the Moon and not the Sun. The Egyptians first conceived the idea of the seasons – each one lasting a period of three months.

The Sun is seen in certain traditions as being a symbol of the soul. Perhaps the correspondence between the heart and the Sun, with the astrological sign of Leo ruling that part of the body, accounts for this.

---

107 Alan Richardson, *Priestess: The Life and Magic of Dion Fortune* (Loughborough: Thoth Publications, 2007) p.316

The soul lies hidden within us and represents a point of stillness, a place where we are centred. The true self is content with its individuality, fulfilled in its own particular purpose. In this sense it is *complete*, uninterested in influencing or even interacting with anything beyond itself. This contradicts the usual view of the solar energy when it is manifest in Leo – one always desiring to attract attention!

The Wisdom of Woman

The Word (*Logos*) is in harmony with Wisdom (*Sophia*). Sophia is the mediator, the interpreter of the Divine Will, a role which she fills to perfection. Sophia is 'The Voice of the Wells', a favourite theme of the medieval troubadours, and represents the *Wisdom of The Grail*. The Philosopher's Stone is the alchemical term for this wisdom and, is often known as the Sophistical Stone.

The essence of both 'Marys' – The Virgin Mary and Mary Magdalene – is to be found within the character of Sophia. Sophia embraces the spiritual and the material, and in doing so attempts to reconcile what has been seen for far too long as an irredeemable conflict. Mary the Virgin was only grudgingly accepted by the Church of England, while Mary Magdalene was the *bête-noir* of both the Catholic and the Protestant faith. Wrongly castigated by the Church Fathers, whose prejudice was only exceeded by their ignorance, Mary Magdalene has finally emerged for her true worth. She is the Bride of Christ. It is within the Grail, and behind the veil of Isis, that such great secrets have been preserved for so long.

Isis reveals herself to only a few, and those fortunate beings are aware that they are in the presence of the Divine Goddess. It is no wonder that the profane are denied this honour, for even the devout must be of stout heart and unshakeable faith, to withstand such an experience. Isis causes the manifestation of the material from out of the astral realms. All is in her image; all that can be seen upon the material plane is but the vision of the Goddess. The munificence – the eternal wisdom of the Goddess – is in all things.

If we study closely the Tarot cards of The Magician and The High Priestess, we note that the magician is standing because he *dares;* the priestess is seated because she *knows*. We may also deduce that the magician is capable of changing his identity and becoming as one with his female counterpart. His willingness to surrender to the feminine aspect indicates that the magician has successfully incorporated heaven and earth. In so doing he announces to the universe that he is fulfilled and whole – a singular character, one to be praised!

It is said that the High Priestess reflects the Magician in that she demonstrates 'How wisdom builds her house' – as the magical adage has it. The most significant feature of that construction from a magical point of view is the pillar that is each side of her. The black pillar on her right is inscribed *Boaz*, and the white pillar to her left, *Jachin*. These depict the pillars that were once part of the Temple of Solomon in Jerusalem; the meaning of the names is obscure.

In the High Priestess card, one may just glimpse the water beyond the Veil. As Isis, the figure has control over all things feminine, as the 'spirit upon the waters'. As Dion Fortune succinctly states, 'All gods are one God, and all Goddesses are one Goddess, and there is one Initiator.' It is only the magician who is permitted to pass beyond the veil of the High Priestess. The magician is her priest and partner and she loves him with great devotion, more than any other mortal in this world.

The energy created by the interaction between these two figures provides fuel for any magical working. In any relationship, this is the key to harmony, advocating the *blending* of the sexes and not a confrontation between the two. Dion Fortune speaks also of 'The begettings and matings of the gods and goddesses, by no means always in holy wedlock...' [108] and, as always, she makes an important point.

When an initiate passes *between* these pillars in a ritual it is a solemn moment. Permission being given to do this implies that the initiate has been granted the right to journey further into the Mysteries. Much significance is attached to this symbolic act and the elements therein. The *space between the two pillars* is perhaps the most highly charged of these. W.G.Gray, with typical candour, describes the arrangement as 'this, that, and the other'. The 'other' – the gap – is shielded from the outer world by the two pillars, and is thus is a most sacred space.

Power is most concentrated in this gap. Energy flows backwards and forwards – from the Inner Temple into the Outer Temple – and also in reverse. For ritual work Gray recommends a password to allow

---

108 Fortune, *ibid.*, p.284

entry here, so that no unwanted entities may pass either in or out. He maintains that sometimes the most malicious demons to be found are in human shape! The Watcher may also stand here in the role of guardian and may ask a relevant question to which the correct answer must be given before entry is permitted.

A 'portal' into another world is an extremely potent image and with practice the magician may summon up this concept whenever he wishes. Portals are to be found at sacred sites, and within the Inner Planes. Magical methods achieve entry to a state of non-existence, one that is never far away from the state of *being* that which we refer to as consciousness. As would be expected, we pass from darkness into light. If we do not wish some other person to pass between these symbolic pillars then we raise our palms, holding flat towards the intruder. The gesture is self-explanatory – it means 'No Entry'.

Jung, citing folklore, said that every man carries his Eve within him. The ignorant man does not recognise the power that naturally resides in womankind and thus abuses or fears her. Accepting the ways of the feminine psyche is not always an easy task. The moods of womanhood may appear, to the rational male mind, to be merely random behaviour. The ways of love naturally reside in the feminine world. Pascal must have been referring to the female heart when he so memorably wrote, 'The heart has reasons that reason cannot know.'

Jung, with his penchant for combining archetypal and mythological figures explains that,

> Salomé is an anima figure. She is bland because she does not see the meaning of things. Elijah is the figure of the wise old prophet and represents the factor of intelligence and knowledge; Salomé, the erotic element. One might say that the two figures are personifications of Logos and Eros.[109]

In this relationship between the two denizens of the temple, the assumption of a god-form by the priest, and the acceptance of that god-form by the priestess take place. In a sacred and secret ritual the priestess physically allows the priest into her body. In this way Man makes Woman fertile upon the earthly plane, while the two sexes meet upon the Inner Planes as the Goddess and the 'sun king'.

---

109 Wehr, *ibid.*, p.298

The Goddess *recognises* the power of the king, yet will only respect him if he is the true guardian of her kingdom. The earthly kingdom *is* woman, as the Celtic priests knew so well, and the Great Mother protects her own. Those who the Goddess loves she blesses, and those upon whom she bestows her love are devoted to her for all time.

Her followers will enjoy bliss in the next world, for the Goddess is present at the moment of Death, for that is also a power she has been given.[110] As she is the Creator so she is the Destroyer, hence the underserved reputation of woman for perpetrating evil. Is it any wonder that in her terrible aspect she is impossible to placate! 'Hell hath no fury like woman scorned' as the old adage goes.

So it can be seen that the fundamental key to the relationship between priest and priestess is love. It is the way of love at its highest, when respect and a sincere equality are never absent. Alan Richardson sounds an ironic note when he suggests that,

> …the irony that all magicians come to appreciate: you can be a mighty Adept, you can, you can see into the souls of men, commune with Masters, project your consciousness across the starry heavens and summon spirits from the vasty deep…but when Love goes wrong, you can be as bewildered and hurt as any teenager.[111]

---

110 It is an interesting debate as to the sex of Death. The Tarot Death is obviously male. Kali and Nephthys are female.
111 Richardson, *ibid.*, p.266

10

The Purpose of Magic

The task of a Magus is to make his word, the expression of his will, come true. It is the most formidable labour that the mind can conceive.

Aleister Crowley

In our so-called 'New Age', it is quite possible to encounter individuals who refer to themselves as 'magicians'. In a 'spiritual centre' such as Glastonbury or Salem, their kind are probably two-a-penny. The *real* magician is indeed a very rare breed and hardly ever encountered. If the student finds himself in the company of the genuine article then he should count himself most fortunate and learn all that he may.

A real practitioner positively oozes magic from every pore, and there is an uncanny feeling that he is 'there and not there' simultaneously. The presence of magic is so strong that by tuning in to his aura one is able to travel with the magus into hitherto unknown places. If you are lucky you may even come back!

The tradition of the magician being also a man of espionage (thinly disguised as diplomat) is most apposite. John Dee and Paracelsus were both successful in this dual role. And is it so much of a contradiction? In contemporary society it would have been a necessity to have been clandestine about magical practice – so why not conceal state secrets as well? In the twenty-first century, surrounded as we are by a constant flood of information, it is almost impossible that 'the facts' will be denied to us.

As the material world, with its 'rationality' and cynicism, looms larger in the collective unconscious, the appeal of the Inner World increases by the same degree. The images in that kingdom have become more vivid, the archetypes more powerful. Upon the Inner Planes, the Magician has gained a position of enormous power. Much is made of 'personal development' these days. Working on our *selves*, diligently and honestly making changes in our perceptions is the most valuable contribution we can make to our well-being. As it was written in the Temple of Apollo at Delphi, *Gnothi Seauton* – Know thyself. The epithet continues – *and thou shall know all the mysteries of the gods and the universe.*

The generation that gave us Dion Fortune, Colonel Seymour and later Bill Gray is long gone, yet their magical power still prevails. They aligned themselves with an earlier tradition, one that encompassed Eliphas Levi, Madame Blavatsky, and The Golden Dawn. The student would do well to heed the approach to magic that was held by these practitioners, and discover for himself the well that true occult knowledge is drawn from.

Aleister Crowley is another authority on magical practice and his writings, when he is not being spurious or verbose, are worthy of study. Crowley certainly knew his magic and was a formidable writer on the subject. As a man with a formidable intellect he always defends his corner vigorously and his dedication to the magical cause can never ever be doubted. Regarded away from the glamour of 'magick', he had some admirable traits and some awful ones. *Crowleyism*, that is, avidly following the more unsavoury aspects of the Great Beast, is something else entirely[112] and a subject so tedious as hardly worth discussing.

A problem for many people who encounter Crowley's writings is that his behaviour on this plane differs so greatly from his magical life. He considered that nothing should stand in the way of 'The Great Work'. An admirable sentiment in itself, but Crowley undoubtedly treated others with scant regard for their welfare or, indeed, their feelings. He was not a very nice person, and it is very likely that his company would have been quite unbearable.

---

112 This aping of a lifestyle is reminiscent of the adulation that surrounded jazz musician Charlie Parker in the 1940s. His devotees appeared to believe that by taking heroin anyone could gain mastery of the saxophone. Similarly by practising various perversions one becomes adept at magic? Absolutely false!

Good and Evil

As one Victorian writer put it, 'Evil is the subject of an appalling quantity of barren speculation.' To insist that God has judged a man to be evil because of his actions, as some pious parties maintain, is blatantly untrue. If we decide to condemn an individual because he has contravened our moral code, that is a responsibility we must take upon ourselves, it is nothing whatsoever to do with God.

Kathryn Schulz speaks of 'the Evil Assumption',

> ...that people who disagree with us are not ignorant of the truth and not unable to comprehend it, but have wilfully turned their backs on it.[113]

Manichaean theology takes the view that evil opposes God, thus removing the omnipotence of the Creator. It is a dualistic view, one that absolves God of any responsibility for the existence of 'evil'. Manichaean doctrine insists that some other entity (Satan) is responsible for any wrong-doing by Man. It is a flawed argument and one that fell out of favour – considered a heresy by the more powerful 'Church' – more than a millennium ago.

The magician favours a wholly different thesis, as has been discussed. If we accept that God created the universe and all things within in it, including the world, God must, by definition be both *good and evil*. He is also just and unjust, merciful and cruel, limitless and limited, unknowable and knowable. All these things, which contain their opposites, unite to form a greater whole which we refer to as God.

It could be suggested that we have a duty to resist evil, and that if we do not do so then we condemn the innocent to being the victims of its acts. The heroic king tirelessly strives against the oppressor of his people. He rejects the opinion of Boethius – *Omnem bonam prorsus esse fortunam* – 'All fortune certainly is good', and takes the responsibility upon himself to vanquish his enemies. But the magician is not a king, his power resides in another realm, one not of this world – even though the effects of his magic may manifest upon the earthly plane.

As has already been posited, *polarity* is a magical concept fundamental to the student's understanding. Opposing natures are

---

113 Kathryn Schulz, *Being Wrong – Adventures in the margin of error* (Portobello, 2011) p.76

necessary for *balance* and that equipoise is a necessity for the practice of magic. Balance is also a necessary part of the character of the magician. His character should combine the nature of each of the four elements, viz. *Air – to Will, Fire – to Dare, Water – to be Silent, and Earth – to Know.* The magical laws of polarity and synthesis are contained within this thesis.

Magic strives to open up channels of communication for particular purposes. For W.G.Gray, developing contact with higher beings held the best possible intent for the practitioner. With practice and devotion a clearer, purer vision of the world emerges. The development and training of the *magical imagination* ensures that, 'the senses will begin to apprehend the realm of celestial forms and images…'[114]

Being a magician guarantees nothing – no favours from providence, and no power to prevent the workings of destiny upon another. No one may escape the ways of *karma*. The magician however, by working 'with the tides rather than against them', seems to be better placed than most to act 'impeccably'. In a world where personal freedom is constantly being threatened by those in power who would wish to determine how others think, the magician is better placed to avoid such a fate than most. As G. de Purucker explains,

> Karma is…essentially a chain of causation, stretching back into the infinity of the past and therefore necessarily destined to stretch into the infinity of the future…Since everything is interlocked and interlinked with everything else, and no thing and no being can live unto itself alone, other entities are of necessity, in smaller or larger degree, affected by the causes or motions initiated by any individual entity…by acting with nature's own great and underlying energies, he puts himself in unison or harmony therewith and therefore becomes a co-worker with nature as the gods are.[115]

With this in mind, '*Be good to yourself*' is commonsense advice. Do nothing detrimental to the physical or mental body, and take regular exercise. This awareness of good health can be extended to the food we eat, the company we keep and what we allow to enter our consciousness. The words that we read before sleep are important, as they set the tone for our dreams and meditations.

---

114 Gray, *ibid.*, p.98
115 G de Purucker, *The Occult Glossary* (London: Rider, 1933) p.165

As his understanding becomes deeper the initiate will discover that he is often aware of being poised between worlds. On occasions he might wonder if he hovers between a state of life and death. The world that appears after our physical death is the reverse of the one that we experience on this plane. It is like a photographic negative; the original image is still recognizable, yet all is transformed. Death is simply another dimension, one of the many that exist. After a time the student will realise that in this realm also resides magical energies – power that may be used for magical practice.

The magician must absorb the wisdom gained from his *past lives* and be thankful for the strength and support of the ancestors. These vibrations serve only to aid him and make less arduous his path. Not all are given to embrace magic, so let those who are chosen regard themselves as being blessed and use their gifts well. Total and utter commitment to the cause of magic is a required of the magician, nothing less will do.

The magical path is certainly not suitable for the faint-hearted or lackadaisical. Every moment spent in its practice should reflect intent. Thoughts should be guided by inner light and actions by the higher self. The magician is the guardian of the past and the future, using his power to strengthen the harmony of the universe. A magician, because he is not proud or envious, rejoices in the triumphs of others. That is his way of demonstrating his absolute regard for the wonder and beauty of creation.

Magic is enhanced by the situation that the magician finds himself in and vice versa. If 'the vibes' are right, then the chances are the magician's power will increase. It is like a cricketer feeling certain that when he goes out to bat it will be 'his day' and that he is quite capable of scoring a century. It is all a question of being master of the situation, and for the magician it is a sense of knowing he may 'alter consciousness at will'[116].

Personal Power

How power is regarded by one who possesses it determines the effect it will have upon that individual. The tyrant is drunk with the prospect of causing havoc and suffering, and the very force that he employs to

---

116 Dion Fortune's oft-quoted definition of magic, 'to effect changes in consciousness in conformity with will'.

reap this evil harvest will eventually destroy him. The magician regards the power that is bestowed upon him as emanating from the universe; it is all around him, invisible, eternal and munificent. In this way, this 'magical capability' is never burdensome to him for he is intimately aware of its origin; he plainly sees its nature.

No matter how wise he may consider himself, at some time or another, every magician is tempted to use their power in a manner which may be wrong. Such a renowned magus as Alan Richardson admitted in a recent interview that in his youth he had sought power – his hormones almost demanding it. He quickly discovered that playing with fire results in burnt fingers. Magical force is autonomous, it may be effective for whatever purpose it is used. Any force however – be it negative or positive – cannot continue for ever, the ultimate rhythm of the universe ensures that.

The powers of darkness emanate from the void of chaos, and are thus uncontrollable. In the Egyptian pantheon the deity Geb rules over these forces, yet they are far more ancient even than him. They represent an implacable, intemperate energy, one that is capable of destroying a man as easily as he himself might swat a fly.

Shiva (the Destroyer of Eastern tradition) is allied, as is Set, with Typhon, and the son of Gaia. The biggest and most fearsome of all creatures, 'the father of all monsters',[117] he was reputedly as tall as the stars, and his hands had each a hundred dragons' heads upon them. He is the chthonic figure of volcanoes, a mighty enemy eventually defeated by Zeus and cast into Tartarus.

There is something of the 'diabolic' about these entities, unfettered spirits that tear matter apart. Among the Egyptian deities, the role assigned to Set embodies this 'non-being'. Those who have chosen to work with ancient gods or discarnate demons realise very quickly that these forces come from a realm far beyond the 'earth magic' that one is likely to encounter at Neolithic sites. The following encounter, recalled by a psychic, suggests that even the apparently benign forces encountered there may sometimes be manifested in quite terrifying ways.

> ...a huge electrical charge in the air (which) rooted me to the spot. I first saw a head form from the soul in front of me in the barrow. A twisted

---

117 He was the father of the Sphinx and Cerberus.

face came out in three dimensions from the earth itself before shrinking back. In its place there formed a being of light approximately the size and girth of a pylon. He was standing on top of the mound itself…and he wasn't happy…[118]

Similarly, those self-styled 'pagans' who attempt to evoke Pan risk evoking forces that they cannot possibly control. Such an unbridled energy will instantly create an imbalance within the individual that is extremely dangerous to their well-being.

Colonel C.R.F. Seymour, an occultist of similar standing to Dion Fortune, wrote extensively upon the 'old gods' and mentions the 'Earth Memory congruous to hidden records buried deep in (the) subconscious mind'[119]

He warns that anyone who attempts to contact 'old gods' may awaken this 'Earth Memory' and that 'the experience may leave him badly shaken mentally and physically'. Eternal entities, archetypes of the collective unconscious created in a time even before the ancients – these are 'the gods before the gods.'

Existing in this realm are the echoes of the kind of forces that Merlin successfully harnessed to use in his magical work. The wizard drew his power directly from the Earth, and his skill went far beyond the practice of evocation. Merlin was so devoted to the divine creation of the cosmos that he was as the creator himself. It is one of the first expositions of man becoming as a god, and thus regarding creation – the material plane that he perceives – to do with as he wished. He was as a colossus of magic because he was so loyal to his calling that magic would always do his bidding and never failed him.

In a subtle way, Merlin was the instrument of the divine will in his encounter with Nimuë – the Lady of the Lake. Merlin taught her the very enchantments that she would use to entrap him! He was aware that the power of the Goddess was about to supersede the old magic, of which he was representative. He chose to sacrifice himself to the will of the universe.

Castaneda's Don Juan explains to his pupil about the *will* and its link to 'personal power'. Here, the shamanic view of magic *is* applicable to the Western way. Don Juan advocates 'knowledge' as power – the

---

118 Richardson, *ibid.*, p.175
119 C.R.F. Seymour, *The Forgotten Mage: Magical Lectures* (Loughborough: Thoth, 1986) p.178

perception of extraordinary phenomena and the acceptance that these things are part of the sorcerer's world. By applying the will, with reference to this knowledge, enables the warrior[120] to 'perform extraordinary acts'. The test of faith in the shamanic tradition is the conviction the warrior must own that he is capable of exercising this will.

Don Juan makes much of the warrior acting in an 'impeccable' manner, and the true magician cannot act in any other way, he is bound by his calling. The universe, recognizing that he is the servant of God, will always come to his aid. The magician has too the same *raison d'être* as the artist, he is content with the act of creation alone; the consideration of any reward is almost irrelevant.

The Magical Tradition

Magic is not a diversion; it is a commitment to a code of behaviour and an approach to life. The magician has the advantage that while he 'still maintains something of the illusion of self, (he is) creating different kinds of illusion'.[121] The magician strives as much as possible to be part of the *Universal Mind*, understanding that:

> …our thoughts generate the physical world just as God is said to have used the power of thought to generate the light and sound that manifested as the Universe.[122]

So are these realms that the student seeks to visit available only to chosen few? Certainly an entirely new approach to seeing the world has to be established, one that has enough breadth to encompass all manner of happenings and phenomena. Rodney Collin is describing an approach to knowledge which may appear to apply only to formal learning, but it has an acute relevance to magic.

> Schools of the fourth way have existed and exist just as the three traditional ways existed and exist. But they are much more difficult to detect, because – unlike the others – they cannot be recognized by any one practice, one method, one task, or one name. They are always inventing new methods,

---

120 Don Juan refers to the 'man of knowledge' as a warrior.
121 Versluis, *ibid.*, p.14
122 Silva, *ibid.*, p.298

new practices, suitable to the time and conditions in which they exist, and when they have achieved one task ... they pass on to another, often changing their name and whole appearance in the process.[123]

The capability of the human brain is truly extraordinary. A pinhead of DNA has the capacity to store the information contained in a pile of books five hundred times the distance from the Earth to the Moon. The brain is a billion times better equipped than the hard drive of any computer. In relaying information, the brain has the advantage over any electronic device because it possesses a more complex mode of operation. The brain has trillions of connections between its cells and is thus capable of performing countless operations simultaneously.

The brain is an organ like any other in the body. The 'mind' is a convenient way of describing the sensations that occur when the brain is in operation. A distinction lies between 'consciousness' and 'perception'. The former applies to a state of experiencing existence, the latter to the mechanics of a particular phenomenon within that experience.

How do we 'perceive' anything? Understanding the mechanics of perception has always been a problem for cognitive science. This area of the brain's activity is regarded as being almost akin to a jungle, one with almost unfathomable depths and no boundaries. How does the brain sort, codify and draw meaning from the information it receives from the senses? Not only that, perception also includes the ability to recognize, detect and understand.

Thus the magician must question any notion of a fixed reality, if not abandon it altogether. Chuang Tsu once wrote,

> I dreamt I was a butterfly. When I awoke, I was not sure whether I was a man who had dreamed I was a butterfly, or a butterfly now dreaming I was a man.[124]

Opening the 'doors of perception' is the first task for those starting out upon the path of magic. A combination of concentration, faith and commitment is needed, and the most important task is to remove the perceptions we have inherited. Prejudice and misinformation abound! Don Juan's pupil recalls:

---

123 Rodney Collin, *The Theory of Celestial Influence* (London: Penguin, 1997) p.201
124 Chuang Tsu (B.Watson trs), *Inner writings* (New York: Harper Collins, 1964)
　　p.324

I always felt as if a veil had been lifted from my eyes, as if I had been partially blind before and now I could see. The freedom, the sheer joy that used to possess me on those occasions cannot be compared with anything else I have ever experienced.[125]

The realisation that there is more to the world than the majority could ever begin to realise, is the first step in understanding it. Everyone is capable of acquiring a supernatural relationship with the natural world but few choose, or are chosen, to do so. As Khalil Gibran reminds us, 'The strangest things are the closest to the real truth.'[126] Yet most people make the error of regarding this inner, invisible world as being irrelevant to the conscious world which they *appear* to perceive so clearly.

Does anyone actually posses the power to alter the nature of reality? Can this be achieved simply by changing the way we regard our own existence? If our conception of the world is based upon our experiences of it, then should we not be able to apply that information in a different way, thus to change it?

The nature of a quantum state is that it always has the potential for change, so perhaps this dictum may be applied to our consciousness. We may not be able to make any state of reality cease to exist, but it may be possible to substitute one reality for another. This may happen when that second reality becomes the absolute centre of our focus.

In applying this procedure to the practice of magic, the magician must first *believe totally in his performance*. As Frazer says: 'From the Law of similarity, the magician infers that he can produce any effect he desires merely by imitating it.'[127] By immersing himself in his craft and having an awareness of his every thought and action, the Magus hones that very performance. In the *unconscious* is a record of all that has ever occurred to the individual in this time or any other, and in any dimension. From these *Akashic Records*[128] springs a mysterious force that creates new order. The magician is able to call upon this force to create a world of his own choosing.

---

125 Carlos Castaneda, *The Fire from Within* (New York: Simon & Schuster, 1984) p.xii

126 Kahil Gibran, *Thoughts and Meditations: A Self-Portrait* (New York: Citadel Press, 1990) p.86

127 J.G. Frazer, *The Golden Bough* (London: Macmillan, 1949) p.12

128 From *akasha* – 'sky', 'sprit', and variously described as a 'metaphysical library' or 'The Mind of God'.

The magician travels in the unconscious realms so frequently that he gathers and retains instinctively any wisdom he has acquired there. He employs ritual magic to give these visions a more potent existence. This magical vision may also work on the conscious plane, enhancing everything observed and making it *phenomenal*. Thus, what might appear mundane or unexceptional to someone else, is charged with significance when observed by the magician.

Once an initiate has passed between the pillars in the temple and then beyond the veil, he journeys from darkness into light. His view of the ordinary world is never the same again. As Crowley stated:

> Day by day matter is replaced by Spirit, the human by the divine; ultimately the change will be complete; God manifest in flesh will be his name.[129]

The truly great magician is always poised between *spirit* and *matter* and he will occupy that state until his passing from this world. He has no fear of Death, as he knows it is only another state of being. By liberating himself from anything that might define or limit him, his magical power can only increase.

The *magical landscape* is the 'kingdom of the mind', and we should always be *using* the brain rather than that organ using us. Even if the magician become 'the master of Nature' he still 'remains subject to the realm of causes and effect, himself also subject to the events and influences he brings into play.'[130]

This ease of journeying from one world to another is what separates the magician from his fellows. The material world the magus regards as if he were somewhere else entirely, and on the Inner Planes he travels with a light step as he is not totally attached to that realm either. He is all too aware that in some way he must function on this earthly plane and he does so with the ease of any worldly man. Yet, but for the magician it is also often a case of, 'now you see me – now you don't'. Having said that, the true magician is not involved with mere *legerdemain*.[131]

---

129 Aleister Crowley, *The Confessions: An Autohagiography* (London: Arkana, 1989) p.89

130 Versluis, *ibid.*, p.54

131 More commonly referred to as 'sleight of hand'.

If 'emotion is the most basic form of consciousness',[132] then it is best that feeling is a state of *unconditional love*. A love of the world promotes a view of existence that is not only generous but capable of embracing its many changes. For our magical work we may adapt the adage that the 'right presence of mind...means that the mind...is nowhere attached to any particular place.'[133]

The dictum 'What we are so we become' is never as true as when applied to the magician, whose duty is to the 'pacification and enlightenment of all beings'.[134] Occasionally his methods might seem oblique but he *knows himself* (or should do) and never forgets that his power has been ordained from above. The initiate should regard the state of 'himself' dispassionately and not taking that self too seriously. The ego can be a destructive monster and better that we '...approach our own aura objectively from the outside...rather than subjectively from the inside.'[135]

It is as well to remember that there is as much power in joy and mirth as in sobriety. As Castaneda's Don Juan reminds us concerning the awesome power of magic, 'the only way to counteract the devastating effect of the sorcerers' world was to laugh at it.'[136]

The wise magician 'still maintains something of the illusion of self, (he is) creating different kinds of illusion'.[137] The magician has within his being all that he requires to achieve his ends, and should, to 'save space' in his mind, rid himself of all that is unnecessary or redundant – clinging to one's 'C.V.' is of no practical use. As *Homo sapiens* we come programmed with certain desires and aspirations, mainly the will to survive. Indeed, as we ascend the spiritual ladder we must not ignore the energies of our lower chakras. As Gareth Knight reminds us,

> ...we need to come to terms with these lower 'dynamics', for they are as important, spiritually, as any 'higher' aspirations. The spiritual quest is not a flight from the problems and conditions of the physical world and our roots within it. It is one that seeks understanding and control of this lower world in which we live and move and have our being.[138]

---

132 Versluis, *ibid.*, p.181
133 E. Herrigel, *Zen in the Art of Archery* (New York: Vintage Books, 1989)
134 Versluis, *ibid.*, p.22
135 Knight, *ibid.*, p.49
136 Castaneda, *ibid.*, p.54
137 Versluis, *ibid.*, p.14
138 Knight, *ibid.*, p.50

The universe can be divided into the spiritual, the mental, the astral and the physical. The mental and physical are planes of form, the astral and spiritual are planes of force. Thus the magician strives as much as possible to unite all these aspects and be part of the *Universal Mind*. He understands that,

> ...our thoughts generate the physical world just as God is said to have used the power of thought to generate the light and sound that manifested as the Universe. [139]

Rupert Sheldrake in his researches into the nature and behaviour of plants and animals uses the term *morphic resonance* to describe the influence of like upon like. Our own genetic implant accounts for the habits that we inherit. This legacy, *the logos*, is balanced against the mutable or creative *spirit*, and when the 'divine element' is introduced, a formidable trinity is constructed. This 'God' element even *contains* the other two elements, and becomes the realm of the creative artist. A magician takes all this even a step further and works with the world's soul – the *animus mundi* – wherein lie all archetypes, all gods, and all mystical forms.

The Magical Path

Magic is more ancient than the gods themselves, for it is magic that must be 'the spark of creation'. For the ancients *spirit was the world* and man was simply part of the ethereal whole, blending almost imperceptibly with the divine. [140] Arthur Versluis speaks of:

> ...the 'primordial unity', the Golden Age...spirit and matter, man and nature, celestial and temporal – all are resolved...magic is natural and all nature is magical. [141]

Ultimately it is not formal training in magic that is important; that alone will never guarantee enlightenment into the Mysteries. The

---

139 Da Silva, *ibid.*, p.298
140 Richard Jefferies in *My Secret Life* commented that: 'The supernatural is miscalled, the natural in truth is the real...I can see nothing astonishing in what are called miracles.'
141 Versluis, *ibid.*, p.14

ancient schools were public institutions and anyone might study there, the Inner temple has always been the abode of the chosen. Its members were selected even before they incarnated upon this plane. To those who truly served magic, all was revealed, for the Universal Mind not only embraces, but protects those who seek true wisdom. Eventually the initiate was able to say, 'I have Omnipotence at my command and Eternity at my disposal.'

Paul Brunton, a traveller in Egypt and India in the 1930s, has left us a marvellous description of his own personal epiphany, experienced while sitting in contemplation with his own 'guru', Ramana Maharishi.

> I find myself outside the rim of world consciousness. The planet which has so far harboured me disappears. I am in the midst of an ocean of blazing light…the primeval stuff out of which worlds are created, the first state of matter. It stretches away into untellable infinite space, incredibly alive.[142]

Aside from those who aspire to the Mysteries, the man on the Clapham omnibus would be wise to allow a degree of magic into his life. We remain on the earthly plane so briefly that it is almost our duty as members of an evolving species to discover the secret powers of the universe. It would seem a great tragedy to be content with just a superficial impression of our existence.

For the true magician the art of manifestation is able to attain a new and higher level. He has the power to create every moment of the day and night in any way we desire. Magic generates more magic, building a spiral that rises to the heavens. Every day new phenomena will appear in our lives. These visions will be a reflection of the journeys we have made on the inner planes. All our meditations, rituals and studies facilitate this magical progress. In this way it grows easier not only to journey between the two worlds, but to integrate them.

The time for magic is at hand. We are told that in 2012 the universal consciousness will begin to divide into differing planes of reality. As Valentin Tomberg tells us,

> …there is a climate of expectation in the world – expectation sustained, contemplated and intensified through the course of the centuries. Without being nourished and directed from above, the energy of human

---

142 Dr. Paul Brunton, *A Search in Secret India* (London: Rider, 1934) p.156

expectation alone would have exhausted itself long ago. But it is not exhausted; rather, on the contrary, it is growing. This is because it aspires to a reality and not an illusion.[143]

Here, the nature of Hermes is apposite in embodying a view of magic that is like a child who prefers to play a game of 'let's pretend' rather than adopt the ways of adulthood and reason. An ability to use magic is his version of maturity. The magician embraces the power of *Tiphareth*, the divine child who stands in the heart of solar power. All hail the Magus! His calling is the most magnificent given to man. Unlimited power is bestowed upon him to bring light into the world. As the Book of Proverbs says, pertaining to man '…as he thinketh in his heart so he is'.[144] So it is the responsibility of every one of us to act and speak with good intent, for…

> …words generate actions, and coupled with intent, actions manifest all manner of consequences. This makes every one of us responsible and accountable for what we manifest.[145]

We must always spurn a clichéd view of the world. The corporate mind is stuffed with the mundane and the predictable. Its desire is to impose a quantitative view of all and deny the mysterious essence that is the real heart of our world. Technology blurs the difference between reality and an 'image of reality', thus deception and manipulation may so easily be employed to control the common mind. We become incurious, no longer delighted or surprised by the world.

It is a sinister situation, one that we need to be aware of, and one that should be constantly resisted. We are dominated by the very technology that we once naïvely supposed would be our servant; the microchip rules society. An unstoppable progress has ensured computers, mobile phones and all the rest will now never go away. We live in an era that has the mind as its matrix. Our neurons work at full stretch and we have built a new world, but we have lost the imagination to build our own temple. The digital experience offers unlimited choice, but only as a substitute for invention.

---

143 Valentin Tomberg, *Meditations on the Tarot* (New York: Element Books, 1993) p.89
144 Proverbs 23 : 7
145 Da Silva, *ibid.*, p.308

Our world in the twenty first century is also a miasma of illusions, many of them harmful. It is ironic that the energy expended on denying the existence of magic by many could be so easily used to promote harmony in the world. As Mike Harris states:

> With dedication, belief and (most importantly) a lively sense of humour, magic can be a worthwhile and fulfilling calling. It can't answer all the world's problems, but it can build bridges between human nature and all nature and between a saner today and a happier tomorrow. This alone marks it out as a noble and worthwhile calling.[146]

Those of us who follow the old traditions wonder who will follow us. Should we, like Merlin, retire into a cave with the Treasures of Britain? There we may wait, like Arthur the King, to be called once more.

---

146 Mike Harris, *Merlin's Chess*, p.27

Bibliography

Bagehot, Walter, *The English Constitution* (London: Collins, 1963)

Brunton, Dr. Paul, *A Search in Secret India* (London: Rider, 1934)

Budge, E. Wallis, *Egyptian Magic* (New York: Dover Publications, 1971)

Castaneda, Carlos, *Tales of Power* (London: Hodder & Stoughton, 1975)

Castaneda, Carlos, *A Journey to Ixtlan* (London: The Bodley Head 1972)

Castaneda, Carlos, *The Fire from Within* (New York: Simon & Schuster, 1984)

Cavendish, Richard, *Man Myth and Magic* (1970 Vol. 3)

Cavendish, Richard, *King Arthur & The Grail – The Arthurian Legends and their Meaning* (London: Weidenfeld and Nicholson, 1978)

Collin, Rodney, *The Theory of Celestial Influence* (London: Penguin, 1997)

Corrie, Joan, *ABC of Jung's Psychology* (London: Kegan Paul, 1985)

Crowley, Aleister, *Magic in Theory and Practice* (London: Penguin Arkana, 1987)

Crowley, Aleister, *The Confessions: An Autohagiography* (London: Penguin Arkana, 1987)

Cummings, Brian, & Josipovici, Gabriel (Eds), *The Spirit of England: selected essays by Stephen Medcalf* (Oxford: Oxbow Books, 2010)

Davie, Michael (Ed), *The Diaries of Evelyn Waugh 1911-1965* (London: Penguin, 1984)

Elton, G.Y., *Teaching English* (London: Macmillan, 1934)

Fortune, Dion, *The Mystical Qabalah* (New York, USA: Ibis, 1981)

Fortune, Dion, *Applied Magic and Aspects of Occultism* (London: Harper Collins, 1987)

Fortune, Dion, *The Magical Battle of Britain* (Cheltenham: Skylight Press, 2012)

Fortune, Dion, *Aspects of Occultism* (1962 Wellingborough: The Aquarian Press, 1962)

Frazer, J.G., *The Golden Bough* (London: Macmillan, 1949)

Gibran, Kahil, *Thoughts and Meditations – A Self-Portrait* (New York: Citadel Press, 1990)

Greenfield, Susan A., *The Private Life of the Brain* (London: Allen Lane, 2000)

Gray, W.G., *Magical Ritual Methods* (Cheltenham: Helios Book Service, 1969)

Gray, W.G., *The Ladder of Lights* (Cheltenham: Helios Book Service, 1968)

Gray, W.G., *Working with Inner Light: the Magical Journal of William G. Gray* (Cheltenham: Skylight Press, 2011)

Harris, Mike, *Merlin's Chess* (Company of Avalon CD/Ritemagic)

Herrigel, E., *Zen in the Art of Archery* (New York: Vintage Books, 1989)

Hume, Robert Ernest, *The Thirteen Principal Upanishads, translated from Sanskrit* (Oxford: O.U.P., 1931)

James, William, *Some Problems of Philosophy* (London: Penguin, 1987)

Knight, Gareth, *Magical Images and the Magical Imagination* (Sun Chalice, 1998)

Knight, Gareth, *A History of White Magic* (London: Mowbrays, 1978)

Ouspensky, P.D. *In Search of the Miraculous* (Orlando: Harcourt, 1949)

Percy, Walker, *The Message in the Bottle* (New York: Farrar, Straus and Giroux, 1954)

Purucker, G de, *The Occult Glossary.* (London: Rider, 1933)

Richardson, Alan, *The Magician's Tables – A Complete Book of Correspondences* (London: Godsfield Press, 2007)

Richardson, Alan, *Dancers to the Gods: The Magical Records of Charles Seymour and Christine Hartley 1937-1939* (Wellingborough: The Aquarian Press, 1985)

Richardson, Alan, *Spirits of the Stones – Visions of Sacred Britain* (London: Virgin, 2001)

Alan Richardson, Alan, *Priestess – The Life and Magic of Dion Fortune* (Lougborough: Thoth Publications, 2007)

Rosenblum, Bruce, and Kuttner, Fred, *Quantum Enigma Physics Encounters Consciousness* (London: Duckworth, 2006)

Ross, G. MacDonald, *Occultism and Philosophy in the Seventeenth Century.* Lecture given at The Royal Institute of Philosophy, 1983.

Sadhu, Mounhi, *Concentration* (London: Allen and Unwin, 1963).

Schulz, Kathryn, *Being Wrong – Adventures in the Margin of Error* (New York: Portobello, 2011)

Seymour, C.R.F., The *Forgotten Mage – Magical Lectures* (Loughborough: Thoth Publications, 1986)

Silva, Da, *The Mind and Myth* (Hampton Roads: Charlottesville Virginia, 2002)

Stewart, R.J., *Ceremony and Ritual Magic* (New York: Harper Collins, 1990)

Strong, Gordon, *Merlin – Master of Magick* (Woodbury, Minnesota: Llewellyn 2010)

Strong, Gordon, *Tarot Unveiled* (London: Mutus Liber, 2009)

Strong, Gordon, *Sun God, Moon Maiden – The Secret World of The Holy Grail* (London: Mutus Liber, 2011)

Swedenborg, Emanuel, *The True Christian Religion*, (Stockholm: Swedenborg Society, 1890)

Tomberg, Valentin, *Meditations on the Tarot* (New York: Element Books, 1993)

Tsu, Chuang (B.Watson trs), *Inner writings* (New York: Harper Collins, 1964)

Versluis, Arthur, *The Philosophy of Magic* (London: Routledge and Kegan Paul, 1986)

Wehr, Gerhard, *Jung – A Biography* (Boston: Shambhala, 2001)

Index

www.ingramcontent.com/pod-product-compliance
Lightning Source LLC
Chambersburg PA
CBHW032005080426
42735CB00007B/516